USE YOUR WORDS

Word Power Quizzes
and **Quotable Quotes**
from America's Most Popular Magazine

Reader's
Digest

New York / Montreal

A READER'S DIGEST BOOK

© 2019 Trusted Media Brands, Inc.

All rights reserved. Unauthorized reproduction,
in any manner, is prohibited.

Reader's Digest is a registered trademark of
Trusted Media Brands, Inc.

ISBN 978-1-62145-423-6

We are committed to both the quality of our products and the
service we provide to our customers. We value your comments,
so please feel free to contact us.

Reader's Digest Adult Trade Publishing
44 South Broadway
White Plains, NY 10601

For more Reader's Digest products and information,
visit our website:
www.rd.com

Printed in China

1 3 5 7 9 10 8 6 4 2

Illustrations copyright ©
Jill Calder, pp. 9, 10, 15, 16, 95, 96, 123, 124, 173, 174
Luc Melanson, pp. 37, 38, 69, 70, 73, 74, 91, 92, 99, 100, 119, 120, 127, 128, 149, 150, 201, 202
Edwin Fotheringham, pp. 39, 40, 43, 44, 65, 66, 141, 142, 197, 198
Ingo Fast, pp. 115, 116, 145, 146, 153, 154, 167, 168, 177, 178 193, 194

Word Power Quiz copyright © by Emily Cox and Henry Rathvon, except
"In Words We Trust," © by Paul Silverman (p. 37); "Words of Yesteryear," © by Alison Ramsey
(p. 73); "Decorating Tips," © by Alison Ramsey (p. 119); "Solar Powered," © by Joan Page
McKenna (p. 201)

CONTENTS

> You'll never have any mental
> muscle if you don't have any
> heavy stuff to pick up.

—DIANE LANE

Words matter more than ever in today's world, and we at *Reader's Digest* have a long history of sharing words and their meanings with our readers. Two beloved features of our magazine, Quotable Quotes and Word Power, are brought together for the first time in this unique package so that we can continue to share with you effective and entertaining ways to use your words.

Whether you are looking for the perfect quote for a special occasion or you are simply working on building your vocabulary to impress people at your next social event, you'll find the ideal words right here in these pages. We've combed the archives to pull the funniest and pithiest quotes for all occasions—from family gatherings to political speeches to celebrations of personal milestones—so you'll always feel that you have just the right words at your fingertips. Drawn from books, interviews, speeches, and television shows, these words of wisdom from actors, politicians, scientists, and other thought leaders reflect the diversity of our world and yet ultimately highlight the ways in which we are tied together by profound, humorous, and universal sentiments. Whether we are laughing at the ways children upend our routines, commiserating about heartbreak, or striving to find ways to age gracefully, we find common ground in words that reflect the human experience.

And while we are inspired by words from those we think are more eloquent than we are, we also know that our readers enjoy the challenge of testing their own ways with words. So we've gathered some of our best Word Power quizzes to give you the opportunity to enrich your own vocabulary. With more than fifty quizzes that have challenged readers over the years, we'll help you discover the meaning of unfamiliar words, add new or unusual words to your vocabulary, and help you stay up to date on new words entering the lexicon. Just ask fans of the hit musical *Hamilton* how inimitable it feels to be complicit in the success of a show about manumission, and you'll be on your way to becoming a Word Power expert (see p. 45).

We hope you'll love this unique blend of wit and wisdom to stretch your heart plus fun quizzes to strengthen your brain. As Margaret Atwood said, "A word after a word after a word is power." Use your words, find your power, and amuse yourself one-upping friends and family along the way.

The Editors of *Reader's Digest*

I'm not a businessman.
I'm a business, man.

—JAY-Z

THE AMERICAN DREAM

Though we author our own destinies,
we find inspiration in the success stories
of others. By listening to the wisdom
they have accrued, we can build
the next steps into the future.

MAKING IT

Do or do not. There is no try.
—YODA

"

Don't just stand there; make something happen.
—LEE IACOCCA

"

Every success is usually an admission ticket
to a new set of decisions.
—HENRY KISSINGER

"

The key to success?
Work hard, stay focused, and marry a Kennedy.
—ARNOLD SCHWARZENEGGER

"

Success is a lot like a bright, white tuxedo. You feel
terrific when you get it, but then you're desperately
afraid of getting it dirty, of spoiling it in any way.
—CONAN O'BRIEN

"

You only have to do a very few things right in your life—
so long as you don't do too many things wrong.
—WARREN BUFFETT

Anybody who's really successful has doubts.

—JERRY BRUCKHEIMER

There's a ball. There's a hoop. You put the ball through the hoop. That's success.

—KAREEM ABDUL-JABBAR

Success is falling nine times and getting up ten.

—JON BON JOVI

Success is more permanent when you achieve it without destroying your principles.

—WALTER CRONKITE

If you want to be successful, just meditate, man. God will tell you what people need.

—CARLOS SANTANA

There is no point at which you can say, "Well, I'm successful now. I might as well take a nap."

—CARRIE FISHER

Winning depends on where you put your priorities. It's usually best to put them over the fence.

—JASON GIAMBI

If you're willing to fail interestingly,
you tend to succeed interestingly.

—EDWARD ALBEE

"

Celebrate what you've accomplished,
but raise the bar a little higher
each time you succeed.

—MIA HAMM

"

To succeed in life, you need three things:
a wishbone, a backbone, and a funnybone.

—REBA MCENTIRE

"

You have to dream big, wish hard,
and chase after your goals because
no one is going to do it for you.

—CEELO GREEN

Success is a lousy teacher.
It seduces people into thinking
they can't lose.

—BILL GATES

THE RIGHT ATTITUDE

Do not allow people to dim your shine
because they are blinded. Tell them to put on
some sunglasses.

—LADY GAGA

"

Fearlessness is the mother of reinvention.

—ARIANNA HUFFINGTON

"

If you have the choice between humble and
cocky, go with cocky. There's always time
to be humble later, once you've been proven
horrendously, irrevocably wrong.

—KINKY FRIEDMAN

"

It is our responsibilities, not ourselves,
that we should take seriously.

—PETER USTINOV

"

When you're out of willpower,
you can call on stubbornness.

—HENRI MATISSE

@Tawni3469 Here is what is important.
As women we need to support
one another not tear each other down.
Let's lift each other up.

@SUZEORMANSHOW

"

When in doubt, look intelligent.

—GARRISON KEILLOR

"

I go into every game thinking I'm going
to be the hero. I have to, or I wouldn't enjoy it.

—DEREK JETER

"

If you make every game a life-and-death
proposition, you're going to have problems.
For one thing, you'll be dead a lot.

—DEAN SMITH

"

One of the secrets of life is to make
stepping stones out of stumbling blocks.

—JACK PENN

"

I know for sure that what we dwell on is who we become.

—OPRAH

MONEY

What's money? A man is a success if he
gets up in the morning and goes to bed at night
and in between does what he wants to do.

—BOB DYLAN

"

Success should be worn like a t-shirt, not a tuxedo.

—PRIYANKA CHOPRA

"

I don't care how much money you have,
free stuff is always a good thing.

—QUEEN LATIFAH

"

They say everybody gets 15 minutes. I hope I'm just inside
the first minute and the next 14 go really slow.

—TERRENCE HOWARD

🐦 QUOTABLE TWEETS

The greatest commodity to own
is land. It is finite. God is not
making any more of it.

@REALDONALDTRUMP

COVER LETTERS

Real success is finding your lifework
in the work that you love.
—DAVID MCCULLOUGH

"

The work praises the man.
—IRISH PROVERB

"

Just as there are no little people or
unimportant lives, there is no insignificant work.
—ELENA BONNER

"

One of the greatest sources of energy
is pride in what you are doing.
—UNKNOWN

"

The more I want to get something done,
the less I call it work.
—RICHARD BACH

"

Pleasure in the job puts perfection in the work.
—ARISTOTLE

WORDS AT WORK

Roll up your sleeves and punch in for this quiz of on-the-job vocabulary. If the grind wears you down, turn the page for answers.

1. oeuvre ('oo-vruh) *n.*—A: job opening. B: body of work. C: French chef.

2. arduous ('ar-je-wus) *adj.*— A: passionate. B: cheap. C: difficult.

3. bum's rush (bumz rush) *n.*— A: mass retail markdown. B: five o'clock traffic. C: forcible eviction or firing.

4. functionary ('funk-sheh-nar-ee) *n.*—A: jack-of-all-trades. B: number cruncher. C: one who works in a specified capacity or as a government official.

5. remunerate (ri-'myu-neh-rayt) *v.*—A: pay for work. B: do the same job repeatedly. C: break a contract.

6. proletariat (proh-leh-'ter-ee-et) *n.*— A: working class. B: head honcho. C: cowboy skilled with a lasso.

7. indolent ('in-doh-lent) *adj.*— A: unpaid. B: averse to work, lazy. C: migratory.

8. Luddite ('luh-diyt) *n.*—A: one who opposes technological change. B: freelancer. C: bigwig.

9. on spec (on spek) *adv.*—A: with no assurance of payment. B: exactly as planned. C: in a supervisor's role.

10. trouper ('troo-per) *n.*— A: traveling theater actor. B: infantry soldier. C: temp-agency worker.

11. sinecure ('siy-nih-kyur) *n.*— A: herbal healer. B: math faculty. C: cushy job.

12. métier ('met-yay) *n.*—A: fee for services. B: oath of office. C: area of expertise.

13. sedentary ('se-den-ter-ee) *adj.*—A: multitasking. B: mindlessly obedient. C: not physically active.

14. garnishment ('gar-nish-ment) *n.*—A: extra pay. B: withholding of wages. C: job in name only.

15. indentured (in-'den-sherd) *adj.*—A: having perks. B: bound to work. C: illegally employed.

"Words at Work" Answers

1. oeuvre—[B] body of work. *Annie Hall* is my favorite movie in Woody Allen's *oeuvre*.

2. arduous—[C] difficult. Rounding up all 400 guests proved a tad *arduous* for the groom.

3. bum's rush—[C] forcible eviction or firing. Whoever built these wobbly chairs should be given the *bum's rush*.

4. functionary—[C] one who works in a specified capacity or as a government official. A local *functionary* for 20 years, Tyler plans to run for a federal post in 2014.

5. remunerate—[A] pay for work. Which office *remunerates* us for these long-distance deliveries?

6. proletariat—[A] working class. Claire is clearly too aristocratic for the rank-and-file *proletariat*.

7. indolent—[B] averse to work, lazy. Santa is furious with this new generation of *indolent* elves.

8. Luddite—[A] one who opposes technological change. Etymology note: *Luddite* refers originally to 19th-century workmen who destroyed machinery as a protest (they took their name from folkloric rebel Ned Ludd).

9. on spec—[A] with no assurance of payment. Despite the lousy market, we agreed to build the house on *spec*.

10. trouper—[A] traveling theater actor. Darla's first paid gig was as a *trouper* with the national cast of *Annie*.

11. sinecure—[C] cushy job. Carol's uncle is the boss, so she's got a *sinecure* as a paper shuffler.

12. métier—[C] area of expertise. They pay her to sing, but Margot's true *métier* is astrophysics.

13. sedentary—[C] not physically active. Studies warn that your body was not meant to be *sedentary* all day.

14. garnishment—[B] withholding of wages. Half of Troy's salary is in *garnishment* for alimony.

15. indentured—[B] bound to work. Hey, I'm not your *indentured* servant—I quit!

PROGRESS

When springtime buds gallop toward
the summer growing season, we look at words
related to forward movement and progress.
See how much headway you can make,
then proceed to the next page for answers.

1. expedite ('ek-spuh-dite) *v.*—
A: speed along. B: diversify.
C: transport.

2. catalyst ('ka-tuh-lihst) *n.*—
A: great leap. B: milestone.
C: agent of change.

3. anabasis (uh-'na-buh-sis) *n.*—
A: military advance. B:
groundbreaking idea. C: executive
decision.

4. fructify ('fruhk-tuh-fie) *v.*—
A: branch out. B: skyrocket.
C: bear fruit.

5. instigate ('in-stih-gayt) *v.*—
A: incite. B: set goals.
C: enact as law.

6. synergy ('sih-ner-jee) *n.*—
A: enthusiasm for change.
B: combined action. C: lack of drive.

7. watershed ('wah-ter-shed) *n.*—
A: sudden loss. B: turning point.
C: reserve of strength.

8. precipitately (prih-'sih-puh-tayt-
lee) *adv.*—A: very cautiously.
B: sequentially. C: with reckless haste.

9. entrepreneur (ahn-truh-preh-
'nyoor) *n.*—A: gatekeeper.
B: business starter. C: social
climber.

10. stratagem ('stra-tuh-jem) *n.*—
A: level of success. B: smooth move.
C: clever plan.

11. aggrandize (uh-'gran-dize) *v.*—
A: enlarge. B: inspire with words.
C: replace.

12. vaticinate (vuh-'tih-sih-nayt)
v.—A: steer to completion.
B: predict. C: become holier.

13. avant-garde (ah-vahnt-'gard)
adj.—A: fearless. B: on the leading
edge. C: well-planned.

14. incremental (ihn-kruh-'mehn-
tuhl) *adj.*—A: time-saving. B: step-
by-step. C: using brain waves.

15. propagate ('prah-puh-gayt) *v.*—
A: support. B: prosper. C: spread.

"Progress" Answers

1. expedite—[A] speed along. Would a note with Mr. Hamilton's likeness *expedite* the delivery?

2. catalyst—[C] agent of change. The ambassador's speech was the main *catalyst* for this peace agreement.

3. anabasis—[A] military advance. The general's brilliantly planned *anabasis* forced the enemies to retreat.

4. fructify—[C] bear fruit. "Our efforts will *fructify*," said Holmes to Watson, "if we trace these footprints."

5. instigate—[A] incite. My sister is the most argumentative person I know—she's always *instigating* a fight.

6. synergy—[B] combined action. All the king's horses and all the king's men are working in *synergy* to reassemble Humpty Dumpty.

7. watershed—[B] turning point. Kira's divorce was a *watershed* in her life—not long after, she changed careers and moved across the country.

8. precipitately—[C] with reckless haste. In a three-legged race, it is never wise to start *precipitately*.

9. entrepreneur—[B] business starter. An *entrepreneur* even as a toddler, Nicki once sold her dollhouse to a schoolmate for $100.

10. stratagem—[C] clever plan. Harold tried various *stratagems* before he finally caught the raccoon that was eating his garbage.

11. aggrandize—[A] enlarge. Carlos used his hefty bonus to *aggrandize* his collection of Rolex watches.

12. vaticinate—[B] predict. It's so difficult to *vaticinate* the weather this time of year, so I always carry a sweater.

13. avant-garde—[B] on the leading edge. Is Elaine's writing style *avant-garde* or just incoherent?

14. incremental—[B] step-by-step. The pharaoh was impatient with the *incremental* progress on his latest pyramid.

15. propagate—[C] spread. Uncle Joe is having a tough time *propagating* his flat-Earth theory.

GO FARTHER OR GO FURTHER?

These near-synonyms cause a lot of confusion, but here's an easy way to know which to use: If you're talking about measurable, physical distance, use *farther*, as in, "How much farther is the station?" But if you're talking about a figurative distance, use *further*, as in, "If you pester me any further, I won't drive you any farther."

POWER WORDS

You might say we're using strong language. Our vocabulary quiz features words about power—having it, getting it, or lacking it. After flexing your mental muscles, turn to the next page for answers.

1. anneal (uh-'neel) *v.*—A: toughen. B: weaken gradually. C: submit to authority.

2. doughty ('dow-tee) *adj.*— A: hesitant. B: willing to yield power. C: stouthearted.

3. enervated ('eh-nur-vay-ted) *adj.*—A: lacking vigor. B: strengthened. C: glorified.

4. dint (dihnt) *n.*—A: heavyweight. B: power. C: electrical unit.

5. proxy ('prahk-see) *n.*— A: strong liking. B: authority to act for another. C: king's royal guard.

6. thew (thoo) *n.*—A: muscular strength. B: castle wall. C: term of surrender.

7. buttress ('buh-tress) *v.*— A: shore up. B: challenge head-to-head. C: dethrone.

8. preponderate (pre-'pahn-duh-rayt) *v.*—A: seize control. B: influence by insidious means. C: have greater importance.

9. duress (du-'rehss) *n.*— A: queen's sister. B: sovereign rule. C: compulsion by threat.

10. puissant ('pwee-sahnt) *adj.*— A: powerful. B: subdued by fear. C: cowardly.

11. arrogate ('ehr-uh-gayt) *v.*— A: supply with weapons. B: seize unjustly. C: crown.

12. effete (eh-'feet) *adj.*— A: marked by weakness. B: brawny. C: able to get things done.

13. attenuate (uh-'ten-yoo-wayt) *v.*—A: make firmer. B: make longer. C: make weaker.

14. coup (coo) *n.*—A: strong signal. B: head honcho. C: power grab.

15. ex officio (eks uh-'fih-shee-oh) *adj.*—A: out of power. B: by virtue of position. C: abstaining from a vote.

"Power Words" Answers

1. anneal—[A] toughen. Fans of the Chicago Cubs were *annealed* by decades of misery.

2. doughty—[C] stouthearted. Prince Ari was a meek little boy, but he grew up to be a *doughty* warrior.

3. enervated—[A] lacking vigor. My bout with the flu left me *enervated* for weeks.

4. dint—[B] power. Chloe doesn't have an ear for languages, but she has become proficient in German by *dint* of hard work.

5. proxy—[B] authority to act for another. Tweedledum couldn't attend the vote, so he gave Tweedle-dee his *proxy*.

6. thew—[A] muscular strength. That guy Biff is all *thew* and no brains.

7. buttress—[A] shore up. My puny allowance isn't doing much to *buttress* my savings.

8. preponderate—[C] have greater importance. In recent years, online news outlets have begun to *preponderate* over traditional print newspapers.

9. duress—[C] compulsion by threat. Indira will eat broccoli, but only under *duress*.

10. puissant—[A] powerful. Octogenarians can still be plenty *puissant*—think Warren Buffett or Queen Victoria.

11. arrogate—[B] seize unjustly. When my mother comes to visit, she immediately *arrogates* my kitchen.

12. effete—[A] marked by weakness. With every failure, Wile E. Coyote's schemes seem more *effete*.

13. attenuate—[C] make weaker. We wear earplugs to *attenuate* the upstairs neighbors' midnight stomping.

14. coup—[C] power grab. The empress had the two conspirators arrested after their attempted *coup*.

15. ex officio— [B] by virtue of position. All department heads are *ex officio* members of the company softball team.

THE GOLDEN ARCH

Why do we call someone an *archbishop*, an *archduke*, or an *archenemy*? The Greeks gave us *arkhos*, meaning "leader," and we've attached it to things good (*archangel*) and bad (*archfiend*). The ending *–archy* ("rule") appears in the kingly monarchy (*mon-* = "one"), the fatherly patriarchy (*pater-* = "father"), and the chaotic anarchy (*an-* = "without").

STUMPED!

What words perplex us most often? The folks at Merriam-Webster revealed 2012's most frequently searched words on their website, and some of them may surprise you. Answers on the next page.

1. paradigm ('payr-a-diym) *n.*— A: puzzle or problem. B: pattern or archetype. C: fringe.

2. malarkey (muh-'lar-kee) *n.*— A: wild partying. B: foolish talk. C: habitual laziness.

3. ubiquitous (yoo-'bik-wi-tus) *adj.*—A: found everywhere. B: pertaining to a wife. C: spoiling for a fight.

4. hypocrite ('hip-uh-krit) *n.*— A: syringe. B: overstatement. C: phony who acts counter to stated beliefs.

5. louche ('loosh) *adj.*—A: quite comfortable. B: of doubtful morals. C: childlike or naive.

6. didactic (diy-'dak-tik) *adj.*— A: taking bold steps. B: intended to teach. C: shrill as crickets.

7. albeit (awl-'bee-it) *conj.*—A: such as. B: even though. C: because.

8. holistic (hoh-'lis-tik) *adj.*— A: sacred. B: three-dimensional. C: involving entire systems.

9. insidious (in-'sid-ee-uhs) *adj.*— A: treacherous. B: known to a select few. C: coiled like a snake.

10. camaraderie (kahm-'rah-duh-ree) *n.*— A: good fellowship. B: photographic memory. C: odd collection.

11. touché (too-'shay) *inter.*— A: "Bon voyage!" B: "Such is life." C: "Good point."

12. conundrum (kuh-'nun-drum) *n.*—A: monotony. B: riddle. C: instrument in a convent.

13. pragmatic (prag-'ma-tik) *adj.*—A: practical. B: boastful. C: stuck in a rut.

14. esoteric ('es-uh-ter-ik) *adj.*— A: distrustful of foreigners. B: of fossil fuels. C: arcane.

15. schadenfreude ('shah-den-froy-duh) *n.*—A: feeling of déjà vu. B: exact copy. C: taking pleasure in another's misfortune.

"Stumped!" Answers

1. paradigm—[B] pattern or archetype. The wax wings aren't working—I need a new *paradigm* for human flight.

2. malarkey—[B] foolish talk. Tell me why your homework isn't done, and spare me the *malarkey*.

3. ubiquitous—[A] found everywhere. I'm still not sure what the film is about, but the *ubiquitous* posters promoting George Clooney's new movie have made me excited to see it!

4. hypocrite—[C] phony who acts counter to stated beliefs. She lectures us about the importance of promptness and then shows up late, the *hypocrite*!

5. louche—[B] of doubtful morals. If you would prefer a *louche* president, by all means vote for my opponent.

6. didactic—[B] intended to teach. Sarah couldn't discuss being a vegan without going off on *didactic* tangents.

7. albeit—[B] even though. Albeit soaked, Dad seemed to enjoy our water-balloon prank.

8. holistic—[C] involving entire systems. In order to see advances across the board, we need to take a holistic approach to improving our schools.

9. insidious—[A] treacherous. It was rather *insidious* of that wolf to

dress up as my grandmother.

10. camaraderie—[A] good fellowship. Despite a dismal win-loss record, our team has plenty of *camaraderie*.

11. touché—[C] "Good point." After Paul observed that I wouldn't be so broke if I didn't buy Jimmy Choos twice a month, I replied, "*Touché.*"

12. conundrum—[B] riddle. Driving into an Italian town is easy; finding your way out is a *conundrum*.

13. pragmatic—[A] practical. We need something more *pragmatic* than rain dances to water our crops.

14. esoteric—[C] arcane. Our club's secret handshake is so *esoteric* that nobody can remember how to do it.

15. schadenfreude—[C] taking pleasure in another's misfortune. I felt a twinge of *schadenfreude* when the Oscar-winning actor didn't get a coveted part.

CROSSWORD CHAMPS

This month, we feature words from the 2016 American Crossword Puzzle Tournament, an annual contest directed by Will Shortz, crossword editor for the *New York Times*. Competitors encountered these words over eight challenging rounds. If you feel puzzled, peek at the next page for answers.

1. bugbear ('buhg-bair) *n.*—A: petty crime. B: character flaw. C: object of dread.

2. sopor ('soh-puhr) *n.*—A: salty taste. B: deep sleep. C: second-year cadet.

3. parlance ('par-lunts) *n.*— A: manner of speaking. B: secret meeting. C: equality.

4. prate ('prayt) *v.*—A: chatter. B: criticize. C: make a grand show.

5. bireme ('biy-reem) *n.*—A: ancient ship propelled by oars. B: marshy tract. C: case of illogic.

6. tiki ('tee-kee) *n.*—A: kitschy cocktail shaker. B: wooden or stone image of a Polynesian god. C: curry sauce.

7. weir ('wair) *n.*—A: ghost. B: mirror image. C: dam in a stream or river.

8. ovine ('oh-viyn) *adj.*—A: of eggs. B: of sheep. C: of grapes.

9. anathema (uh-'na-thuh-muh) *n.*—A: main topic or theme. B: total opposite. C: someone or something intensely disliked.

10. acolyte ('a-kuh-liyt) *n.*— A: follower. B: spiritual healer. C: circle of stones.

11. vituperate (viy-'too-puh-rayt) *v.*—A: give new life to. B: hiss like a snake. C: use harsh language.

12. lasciviously (luh-'sih-vee-uhs-lce) *adv.*—A: with lust. B: in a careless way. C: snidely.

13. tittle ('tih-tuhl) *n.*—A: dot in writing. B: small songbird. C: mob snitch.

14. auspices ('ahs-pih-sez) *n.*— A: flavorings. B: terms of forgiveness. C: patronage.

15. arboreal (ar-'bor-ee-uhl) *adj.*—A: from the north. B: about winds. C: concerning trees.

"Crossword Champs" Answers

1. bugbear—[C] object of dread. Rain is the biggest *bugbear* for the organizers of our town's annual autumn festival.

2. sopor—[B] deep sleep. Rip Van Winkle wasn't just napp*ing*—he was in a doozy of a *sopor*.

3. parlance—[A] manner of speaking. Juan's keynote speech was "mic drop" good, to use the current *parlance*.

4. prate—[A] chatter. Do you have anything useful to tell me, or are you just *prating* into the air?

5. bireme—[A] ancient ship propelled by oars. Don't the centipede's legs remind you of the oars on a Roman *bireme*?

6. tiki—[B] wooden or stone image of a Polynesian god. I traveled to Maui and returned with a lei, a ukulele, and a wooden *tiki*.

7. weir—*[C]* dam in a stream or river. The river's *weir* helps to prevent flooding.

8. ovine—[B] of sheep. The *ovine* residents of our farm always bleat loudly when they're sheared.

9. anathema—[C] someone or something intensely disliked. I don't mind snakes, but spiders are *anathema*.

10. acolyte—[A] follower. We couldn't even hear the speaker over the chants of his fervent *acolytes*.

11. vituperate—[C] use harsh language. You will get further by being polite than by *vituperating* at full volume.

12. lasciviously—[A] with lust. Ali dipped her finger into the bowl of frosting and then licked it *lasciviously*.

13. tittle—[A] dot in writing. Ryan meticulously dots each i with a perfect *tittle*.

14. auspices—[C] patronage. Under the *auspices* of her mother, little Courtenay has opened a lemonade stand.

15. arboreal—[C] concerning trees. The birds in my backyard prefer their *arboreal* nests to my adorable birdhouses.

FEELING CROSS?

Fans of crosswords may humorously call themselves *cruciverbalists*. This term for puzzle aficionados is stitched together from the Latin *crux* (for "cross") and *verbum* (for "word"). Of course, a tormented solver might point out that *crux* is also at the root of *excruciating* ("painful") and related to *crucible* ("severe test")—and switch to word searches.

TALK LIKE A GENIUS

Does your lexicon need a lift? Try these terms guaranteed to impress even the most well-versed wordsmiths—from the vocabulary-building book *Talk Like a Genius* by Ed Kozak. Stumped? Check the next page for answers.

1. capitulate (kuh-ˈpih-chuh-layt) *v.*—A: provide funding. B: stop resisting. C: state formally.

2. unequivocal (uhn-ih-ˈkwih-vuh-kuhl) *adj.*—A: cool under pressure. B: untamed or out of control. C: leaving no doubt.

3. cavalier (ka-vuh-ˈlir) *adj.*— A: nonchalant or marked by disdainful dismissal. B: dome shaped. C: undefeated or worthy of praise.

4. leery (ˈlir-ee) *adj.*—A: untrusting. B: odd. C: off balance.

5. levity (ˈleh-vuh-tee) *n.*— A: taxation. B: merriment. C: departure.

6. penchant (ˈpen-chunt) *n.*— A: recital. B: strong liking. C: deep thought.

7. bifurcate (ˈbiy-fer-kayt) *v.*— A: tell lies. B: flash like lightning. C: divide into parts.

8. craven (ˈkray-vuhn) *adj.*— A: chiseled. B: needy or famished. C: cowardly.

9. coterie (ˈkoh-tuh-ree) *n.*— A: exclusive group. B: takeover. C: birdcage.

10. stalwart (ˈstahl-wert) *adj.*— A: loyal. B: left-handed. C: disguising one's weakness.

11. travesty (ˈtra-vuh-stee) *n.*— A: wardrobe. B: long journey on foot. C: absurd imitation.

12. hedonism (ˈhee-duh-nih-zuhm) *n.*—A: espionage. B: sun worship. C: pursuit of pleasure.

13. obviate (ˈahb-vee-ayt) *v.*— A: watch over. B: prevent or render unnecessary. C: leave unfinished.

14. excoriate (ek-ˈskor-ee-ayt) *v.*— A: hollow out. B: criticize harshly. C: sketch in detail.

15. penurious (peh-ˈnur-ee-uhs) *adj.*—A: given to fits of rage. B: wordy. C: poor.

"Talk Like a Genius" Answers

1. capitulate—[B] stop resisting. Only when I wrapped the pill in bacon did my dog finally *capitulate*.

2. unequivocal—[C] leaving no doubt. The ump unleashed a resonant, *unequivocal* "Steee-rike!"

3. cavalier—[A] nonchalant or marked by disdainful dismissal. Our driver had a shockingly *cavalier* attitude about the steep mountain road ahead.

4. leery—[A] untrusting. Initially, Eve was a touch *leery* of the apple.

5. levity—[B] merriment. Our family thankfully found moments of *levity* during the memorial.

6. penchant—[B] strong liking. Thomas was warned repeatedly about his *penchant* for daydreaming in meetings.

7. bifurcate—[C] divide into parts. If anything, Donald Trump has certainly managed to *bifurcate* the nation.

8. craven—[C] cowardly. She took a markedly *craven* position against the weak crime bill.

9. coterie—[A] exclusive group. Claire's *coterie* consisted entirely of fellow Mozart enthusiasts and violinists.

10. stalwart—[A] loyal. Throughout the senator's campaign, Kerrie has repeatedly shown *stalwart* support.

11. travesty—[C] absurd imitation. Her lawyer demanded an appeal, calling the jury's decision a *travesty* of justice.

12. hedonism—[C] pursuit of pleasure. In Shakespeare's *Henry IV*, young Prince Hal mistakes *hedonism* for heroism.

13. obviate—[B] prevent or render unnecessary. Gloria's doctor hoped that physical therapy would *obviate* the need for more surgery.

14. excoriate—[B] criticize harshly. Coach Keegan was *excoriated* by the media for the play calling during the game's final minutes.

15. penurious—[C] poor. Paul and Carla entered the casino flush and left it *penurious*.

SMART STORY

If you track down the origins of *intelligence*, you find the Latin *inter* ("between, among") plus *legere* ("choose, read"). To be intelligent, then, is literally "to choose among" or "discern." The versatile *legere* also gives us the words *legend, lecture, election*, and *logo*.

EDUCATION COUNTS

Sharpen your pencil and put on your thinking cap—it's time to head back to school. We've selected a roster of words that will challenge learners of all ages. Will you make the grade or draw a blank? Turn the page for answers.

1. parochial (puh-'roh-kee-uhl) *adj.*—A: rigorous. B: elementary. C: run by a church.

2. conscientious (kon-shee-'en-shuhs) *adj.*—A: extremely careful. B: alert. C: well educated.

3. pore (pohr) *v.*—A: quote at length. B: study intently. C: write by hand.

4. carrel ('kehr-uhl) *n.*—A: library nook. B: songbook. C: punctuation mark.

5. curriculum (kuh-'rih-kyuh-luhm) *n.*—A: lecture hall. B: highest grade. C: set of courses.

6. pedantic (pih-'dan-tik) *adj.*—A: misbehaving. B: making a show of knowledge. C: highly poetic.

7. glean (gleen) *v.*—A: divide equally. B: erase. C: gather.

8. rudiments ('roo-duh-ments) *n.*—A: wrong answers. B: small classes. C: beginner's skills.

9. syntax ('sin-tax) *n.*— A: dictionary. B: sentence structure. C: math equation.

10. semantic (sih-'man-tik) *adj.*— A: related to meaning in language. B: collegiate. C: in essay form.

11. pedagogy ('peh-duh-goh-jee) *n.*—A: art of teaching. B: debate tactic. C: study of children.

12. syllabus ('sih-luh-buhs) *n.*—A: word part. B: class outline. C: textbook.

13. woolgathering ('wool-ga-thuh-ring) *n.*—A: taking notes. B: memorizing. C: daydreaming.

14. cognizant ('cog-nuh-zent) *adj.*—A: engrossed. B: aware. C: automated.

15. empirical (im-'peer-ih-kuhl) *adj.*—A: theoretical. B: quick to learn. C: based on observation.

"Education Counts" Answers

1. parochial—[C] run by a church. Years of wearing *parochial* school uniforms left me hating plaid.

2. conscientious—[A] extremely careful. Carly is so *conscientious*—this sloppy book report isn't like her.

3. pore—[B] study intently. Sam *pored* over his European history notes the night before the midterm.

4. carrel—[A] library nook. In graduate school, I'd practically sleep in a *carrel* before final exams.

5. curriculum—[C] set of courses. The first class in Pierre's cooking *curriculum* is Sauces, Soups, and Stews.

6. pedantic—[B] making a show of knowledge. Professor Riordon knows a lot, but I find his bookish teaching style a bit *pedantic*.

7. glean—[C] gather. From what I *glean* from her essays, Shauna has done a lot of traveling.

8. rudiments—[C] beginner's skills. First-year students at Hogwarts must learn the *rudiments* of wizardry.

9. syntax—[B] sentence structure. This sentence a rather tortured *syntax* has.

10. semantic—[A] related to meaning in language. "What's the *semantic* difference between *clown* and *fool*?" our English teacher asked.

11. pedagogy—[A] art of teaching. "There are no lucrative awards for *pedagogy*," said Mr. Wilcox, "but I find it very rewarding."

12. syllabus—[B] class outline. This *syllabus* has no homework assignments listed—woo-hoo!

13. woolgathering—[C] daydreaming. If you hadn't been *woolgathering* in class, you wouldn't have flunked.

14. cognizant—[B] aware. "I'm *cognizant* of the facts of your case," the vice principal told Mason, "but they don't excuse cheating."

15. empirical—[C] based on observation. Brody's science project presents *empirical* evidence that eating chocolate is good for you.

NONWORKING CLASS

Cramming for tests, slaving over papers—school can be a grind. But the word *school* comes from the Greek *shkole*, meaning "idleness." In ancient Greece, *shkole* referred to how the well-to-do spent their spare time: in philosophical discussion. *Shkole* became the Latin *schola* ("meeting place for teachers and students"), which in turn gave us *school*.

EDUCATION

The whole purpose of education
is to turn mirrors into windows.

—SYDNEY J. HARRIS

"

Education is what survives when what
has been learnt has been forgotten.

—B. F. SKINNER

"

[Learning] is the only thing which the mind
can never exhaust . . . never fear . . . and
never dream of regretting.

—T. H. WHITE

"

I think sleeping was my problem in school.
If school had started at four in the afternoon,
I'd be a college graduate today.

—GEORGE FOREMAN

"

Education's purpose is to replace
an empty mind with an open one.

—MALCOLM FORBES

"

Education is a progressive
discovery of our own ignorance.

—WILL DURANT

GRADUATION SPEECHES

You can't connect the dots looking forward;
you can only connect them looking backward.
So you have to trust that the dots will somehow
connect. You have to trust in something—
your gut, destiny, life, karma.

—STEVE JOBS

"

I was a loser in high school. . . .
And I'm here to tell my fellow dweebs and losers
that your day will come. High school
is not the final word on you. There is hope.

—DOUG MARLETTE

"

How will your experience pave the way
for a new voice in America? I hope it will take
you out these doors, out into the open air.
You will breathe it in your lungs and say,
"From now on, this life will be what I stand for. . . .
Move over—this is my story now."

—JODIE FOSTER

Getting up in the morning and having work
you love is what makes life different for people.
If you get into a position where you don't love what
you're doing, get off it.

—BOB WOODWARD

"

The really important kind of freedom involves
attention and awareness and discipline,
and being able truly to care about other people
and to sacrifice for them over and over in myriad
petty, unsexy ways every day.

—DAVID FOSTER WALLACE

"

The unfortunate, truly exciting thing about
your life is that there is no core curriculum. . . .
So don't worry about your grade or the results
or success. Success is defined in myriad ways, and
you will find it, and people will no longer
be grading you.

—JON STEWART

"

Education and the warm heart—if you combine
these two, then your education, your knowledge,
will be constructive. You are yourself
then becoming a happy person.

—THE DALAI LAMA

There's an old saying about those who forget history. I don't remember it, but it's good.

—STEPHEN COLBERT

PATRIOTIC & PROUD

History is often written by the winners, but the records of what was said reflect the truth more closely. From politicians, protestors, and patriots, the spirit of our time is collected in the words by which we remember our leaders.

AMERICA

America is a vast conspiracy to make you happy.
—**JOHN UPDIKE**

"

America is not just a country. It's an idea.
—**BONO**

"

America is not perfect, but it's much better
than anywhere else in the world.
—**CATHERINE ZETA-JONES**

"

I think the most un-American thing you
can say is "You can't say that."
—**GARRISON KEILLOR**

"

America is so vast that almost everything
said about it is likely to be true, and the opposite
is probably equally true.
—**JAMES T. FARRELL**

"

The great arrogance of the present is to
forget the intelligence of the past.
—**KEN BURNS**

Poker is to cards and games what jazz is to music.
It's this great American thing, born and bred here.
We dig it because everybody can play.

—STEVE LIPSCOMB

"

What is the essence of our America? Finding and
maintaining that perfect, delicate balance
between freedom "to" and freedom "from."

—MARILYN VOS SAVANT

"

You don't have to be old in America to say
of a world you lived in, "That world is gone."

—PEGGY NOONAN

"

Whoever wants to know the heart and mind
of America had better learn baseball.

—JACQUES BARZUN

"

The American dream is not over.
America is an adventure.

—THEODORE WHITE

"

America did not invent human rights.
In a very real sense, it is the other way around.
Human rights invented America.

—JIMMY CARTER

GOVERNMENT

To lodge all power in one party and keep
it there is to insure bad government.
—MARK TWAIN

"
What Washington needs is adult supervision.
—BARACK OBAMA

"
You don't pay taxes—they take taxes.
—CHRIS ROCK

"
It is easier to build strong children
than to repair broken men.
—FREDERICK DOUGLASS

One of the fondest expressions
around is that we can't be the world's
policeman. But guess who gets called
when suddenly someone needs a cop.

—GEN. COLIN POWELL

If we don't believe in free expression for those we despise, we don't believe in it at all.

—NOAM CHOMSKY

Governing a large country is like frying a small fish. You spoil it with too much poking.

—LAO-TZU

"

A little government and a little luck are necessary in life, but only a fool trusts either of them.

—P. J. O'ROURKE

"

Everybody wants to eat at the government's table, but nobody wants to do the dishes.

—WERNER FINCK

"

Government can't give us anything without depriving us of something else.

—HENRY HAZLITT

"

When government accepts responsibility for people, then people no longer take responsibility for themselves.

—GEORGE PATAKI

POLITICS

Politics is the only business where doing
nothing other than making the other guy
look bad is an acceptable outcome.

—MARK WARNER

"

I looked up the word *politics* in the dictionary.
It's actually a combination of two words: poli, which
means many, and tics, which means bloodsuckers.

—JAY LENO

"

Ideas are great arrows, but there has to be
a bow. And politics is the bow of idealism.

—BILL MOYERS

"

Washington, D.C., is to lying what
Wisconsin is to cheese.

—DENNIS MILLER

Everybody knows politics
is a contact sport

—BARACK OBAMA

Take it from me—elections matter.
—AL GORE

It's in the democratic citizen's nature to be like a
leaf that doesn't believe in the tree it's part of.
—DAVID FOSTER WALLACE

"

Disobedience is the true foundation of liberty.
The obedient must be slaves.
—HENRY DAVID THOREAU

"

Politics is the art of looking for trouble,
finding it everywhere, diagnosing it incorrectly,
and applying the wrong remedies.
—GROUCHO MARX

"

I'm older than dirt, I've got more scars
than Frankenstein, but I've learned
a few things along the way.
—JOHN MCCAIN

"

Where you stand should not depend
on where you sit.
—JANE BRYANT QUINN

HISTORY

Each time history repeats itself, the price goes up.
—RONALD WRIGHT

"

Well-behaved women seldom make history.
—LAUREL THATCHER ULRICH

"

The past is a source of knowledge,
and the future is a source of hope.
Love of the past implies faith in the future.
—STEPHEN AMBROSE

"

Live out of your imagination, not your history.
—STEPHEN R. COVEY

🐦 QUOTABLE TWEETS

In a thousand years,
archaeologists will dig up
tanning beds and think
we fried people as punishment.
@OLIVIAWILDE

LEADERSHIP

A leader is one who, out of madness or
goodness, volunteers to take upon himself the
woe of the people. There are few men so foolish,
hence the erratic quality of leadership.

—JOHN UPDIKE

"

Being powerful is like being a lady. If you
have to tell people you are, you aren't.

—MARGARET THATCHER

"

Power is nothing unless you can turn it into influence.

—CONDOLEEZZA RICE

"

You have to have a vision. It's got to be
a vision you articulate clearly and forcefully.
You can't blow an uncertain trumpet.

—REV. THEODORE HESBURGH

"

Most people can bear adversity. But if you wish
to know what a man really is, give him power.

—ROBERT G. INGERSOLL

PROTEST CAMPAIGNS

There may be times when we are powerless
to prevent injustice, but there must never
be a time when we fail to protest.

—ELIE WIESEL

"

What is morally wrong cannot be politically right.

—WILLIAM GLADSTONE

"

To sin by silence when they should protest
makes cowards of men.

—ABRAHAM LINCOLN

"

A small body of determined spirits fired
by an unquenchable faith in their mission can
alter the course of history.

—MAHATMA GANDHI

"

You're not supposed to be so blind with patriotism
that you can't face reality. Wrong is wrong,
no matter who does it or who says it.

—MALCOLM X

IN WORDS WE TRUST

The United States can take credit for scores of contributions to the world's lexicon: Rock 'n' roll, software, teddy bear, and even A-OK are just a few all-American additions. So to celebrate, we've compiled some lesser-known gems with U.S. roots. Answers (plus a little etymology) on next page.

1. borax *n.*—A: cheap or shoddy merchandise, usually furniture. B: wooden dam. C: creature in folklore.

2. highbinder *n.*—A: type of moonshine. B: 19th-century gun. C: corrupt politician or mean person.

3. Holy Joe *n.*—A: meat sandwich. B: clergyman. C: exclamation used in early baseball leagues.

4. spoony *adj.*—A: silly or unduly sentimental. B: drunk. C: slow-witted.

5. alewife *n.*—A: rudimentary log cabin. B: kinship. C: herring common to the Atlantic Coast.

6. blackstrap *n.*—A: type of molasses. B: early horse saddle. C: gambling house.

7. slimsy *adj.*—A: of questionable nature. B: frail. C: slippery.

8. blatherskite *n.*—A: double-edged hunting knife. B: one who speaks nonsense. C: red rock indigenous to North America.

9. sockdolager *n.*—A: decisive blow or answer. B: counselor. C: nickname for a banker.

10. jag *n.*—A: stone step. B: unrestrained activity. C: insult.

11. piker *n.*—A: one who gambles with a small amount of money or does something cheaply. B: one who prefers to walk. C: nickname for a logger.

12. simon-pure *adj.*—A: as fresh as mountain air. B: immoral, from *Uncle Tom's Cabin.* C: of untainted integrity.

13. callithump *n.*—A: boisterous band or parade. B: carnival game. C: rabbit originally found in the Deep South.

14. deadhead *n.*—A: traveler who has not paid for a ticket. B: slang for male witch. C: weed particular to the Florida Everglades.

"In Words We Trust" Answers

1. borax—[A] cheap or shoddy merchandise, usually furniture (probably from New York's Lower East Side; late 1800s). "What a *borax* of a table!" cried Alison as its legs collapsed.

2. highbinder—[C] corrupt politician or mean person (from the Highbinders, bullies in New York City; early 1800s). While not an evil man, the mayor was at the very least a *highbinder*.

3. Holy Joe—[B] clergyman (slang, especially in the U.S. armed forces; 1800s). The anxious privates all went to visit the *Holy Joe* before shipping out.

4. spoony—[A] silly or unduly sentimental (from *spoon*, "foolish person"; early 1800s). Her *spoony* ex tried to win her back with a truckload of tulips.

5. alewife—[C] herring common to the Atlantic Coast (perhaps an alteration of an American Indian name; 1633). Art prefers *alewife* to typical sea herring.

6. blackstrap—[A] type of molasses (from a mixture of rum and molasses; 1800s). Fran's must-have ingredient for his beans? *Blackstrap* molasses.

7. slimsy—[B] frail (blend of *slim* and *flimsy*; 1845). "I can't knit with *that*," Emilie said. "The cotton is so *slimsy*!"

8. blatherskite—[B] one who speaks nonsense (alteration of Scottish *blether*, "blather," and *skate*, "contemptible person"; U.S. usage from the American Revolution). Can't anyone silence that *blatherskite*?!

9. sockdolager—[A] decisive blow or answer (perhaps from *sock*, "to hit hard"; 1827). The variation *sockdologising* is supposedly one of the last words Lincoln heard before being shot.

10. jag—[B] unrestrained activity (from Jack London's *The Valley of the Moon*; 1913). Joy went on a whining *jag* after losing her phone.

11. piker—[A] one who gambles with a small amount of money or does something cheaply (from frugal residents of Pike County, Missouri; mid-1800s). Always the family's *piker*, Ruthie played only three dollars at the craps table.

12. simon-pure—[C] of untainted integrity (from a character in the English play *A Bold Stroke for a Wife*; U.S. usage, 1840s). Her reputation as a writer? She's *simon-pure*.

13. callithump—[A] boisterous band or parade (from *callithumpian band*, "noisemakers on New Year's Eve"; 1800s). At the much-anticipated *callithump*, the Colts celebrated their gridiron win.

14. deadhead—[A] traveler who has not paid for a ticket (at least as far back as 1840s New York City). "Does that *deadhead* really work for the airline?"

WITHIN REGION

The year 2012 marked the long-anticipated completion of the five-volume *Dictionary of American Regional English*. These tomes feature words and phrases, both old and new, that vary from place to place. Here, some of our favorites (we've added the primary regions for each to help you along). Answers on next page.

1. pinkletink *n., Martha's Vineyard*—A: piano. B: light rain shower. C: spring peeper frog.

2. king's ex *exclam., Gulf states, west of Mississippi River*—A: get lost! B: good luck! C: time out!

3. snail *n., California*—A: cinnamon roll. B: boyfriend. C: sound made with the sides of the hands.

4. noodle *v., Arkansas, Missouri, Oklahoma*—A: catch fish bare-handed. B: drink from a flask. C: visit neighbors.

5. silver thaw *n., Oregon, Washington*—A: brook trout. B: freezing rain. C: 50th wedding anniversary.

6. on the carpet *adj., South*—A: under arrest. B: ready to marry. C: exhausted.

7. remuda *n., Southwest*—A: herd of horses. B: dry gulch. C: bunk.

8. punee *n., Hawaii*—A: loose dress. B: couch or sofa. C: outflow of lava.

9. pungle *v., West*—A: bollix. B: pay up. C: make verbal jokes.

10. givey *adj., Mid- and South Atlantic*—A: humid or moist. B: too talkative. C: up for anything.

11. rumpelkammer *n., Wisconsin*—A: thunderstorm. B: storage closet. C: unruly child.

12. mug-up *n., Alaska*—A: mascara kit. B: coffee break. C: robbery.

13. berm *n., West Virginia*—A: shoulder of a road. B: tip jar. C: big poker hand.

14. hook Jack *v., New England*—A: come up empty. B: add cheese to a dish. C: skip school.

15. all-overs *n., South*—A: one-piece suit. B: nervous feelings. C: gossip.

"Within Region" Answers

1. pinkletink—[C] spring peeper frog. By May, the *pinkletinks* are in their full-throated glory.

2. king's ex—[C] time out! As soon as the dentist reached for his drill, Bucky yelled, "*King's ex!*"

3. snail—[A] cinnamon roll. The edge went off my appetite when I found a hair in my favorite bistro's *snail*.

4. noodle—[A] catch fish bare-handed. For a guy who used to *noodle*, Jeremy sure has clumsy mitts.

5. silver thaw—[B] freezing rain. Hoping to lighten the mood, Audrey did her best Gene Kelly, singing and dancing in the *silver thaw*.

6. on the carpet—[B] ready to marry. Max is *on the carpet*, but Grace is still on the fence.

7. remuda—[A] herd of horses. My brother's two kids hit the house during visits like a galloping *remuda*.

8. punee—[B] couch or sofa. Lounging supine on her *punee*, Clare spends the day watching soaps and eating poi chips.

9. pungle—[B] pay up. If you don't *pungle* soon, they're going to send Biff to visit you.

10. givey—[A] humid or moist. The *givey* August weather left us drawn down and listless come midday.

11. rumpelkammer—[B] storage closet. When we played hide-and-seek, nobody could find little Waldo in the *rumpelkammer*.

12. mug-up—[B] coffee break. Maria gets nothing done, because she yaks through a *mug-up* every ten minutes.

13. berm—[A] shoulder of a road. Thoroughly exhausted by the drive from Portland, Alice pulled to the *berm* for a break.

14. hook Jack—[C] skip school. Whenever there's an algebra test, Moe and I *hook Jack* and head for the river.

15. all-overs—[B] nervous feelings. I get the *all-overs* when my brother lets his pet tarantula loose.

SANDWICH SHOP
Match the city with the sandwich name that is common there.

1. New York City	A. grinder
2. Philadelphia	B. po'boy
3. Boston	C. hero
4. New Orleans	D. hoagie
5. Yonkers	E. wedge

1. C; 2. D; 3. A; 4. B; 5. E

AMERICANA

From the land that gave birth to baseball, Budweiser, and bebop, we bring you this homegrown mix of words, phrases, and names. Need help with your Americana? Ask your uncle Sam—or check the next page for answers.

1. pompadour ('pahm-puh-dohr) *n.*—A: parade uniform. B: convertible top. C: men's hairstyle.

2. El Capitan (ehl 'kahp-ee-'tahn) *n.*—A: Alamo general. B: Yosemite rock formation. C: Civil War stronghold.

3. jackalope ('jak-uh-lohp) *n.*— A: rabbit with antlers. B: rodeo bronco. C: crusading journalist.

4. barnstorm ('barn-storm) *v.*— A: travel around performing. B: dance at a hoedown. C: give a ranting speech.

5. ponderosa (pahn-deh-'roh-suh) *n.*—A: gold mine. B: pine tree. C: mountain range.

6. fake book ('fayk book) *n.*— A: recipe folder or container. B: stack of marked playing cards. C: collection of songs.

7. tricorn ('try-korn) *adj.*— A: popped, as in kernels. B: deliberately campy. C: like Paul Revere's hat.

8. bunting ('buhn-ting) *n.*— A: fabric for flags. B: baby boy. C: Roaring Twenties dress.

9. Tin Pan Alley (tihn pan 'a-lee) *n.*—A: hideout for hoboes. B: row of factories. C: pop music center formed in the late 19th century.

10. twain ('twayn) *n.*—A: disguise. B: male suitor. C: two.

11. moxie ('mahk-see) *n.*— A: chorus girl. B: courage. C: double-talk or deceptive message.

12. brushback ('bruhsh-bak) *n.*— A: grooming technique for a horse. B: baseball pitch. C: method of sawing or logging.

13. eighty-six ('ay-tee 'siks) *v.*— A: round up. B: get rid of. C: submerge.

14. copacetic (koh-puh-'seh-tik) *adj.*—A: very satisfactory. B: satirical. C: pepped up.

"Americana" Answers

1. pompadour—[C] men's hairstyle. The piled-up-in-front do, notably worn by Elvis, was named for France's Madame de Pompadour (1721–1764).

2. El Capitan—[B] Yosemite rock formation. It's Spanish for "the captain"—appropriate, since the landmark impressed early explorers as the dominant rock in the valley.

3. jackalope—[A] rabbit with antlers. In Wild West folklore, it's a cross between a jackrabbit and an antelope.

4. barnstorm—[A] travel around performing. Semipro baseball teams used to tour the country playing exhibition games in their off-season.

5. ponderosa—[B] pine tree. The name of this heavy western North American tree has roots (pun intended) in the word *ponderous*.

6. fake book—[C] collection of songs. Used by jazz and other musicians to quickly learn songs, it has bare-bones melody lines and chord names.

7. tricorn—[C] like Paul Revere's hat. A tricorn hat is bent at three points (*tri* for "three" plus *corn* for "corner").

8. bunting—[A] fabric for flags. Made of worsted wool, it is typically used for Fourth of July banners.

9. Tin Pan Alley—[C] pop music center formed in the late 19th century. It was named for the tinkling pianos in a neighborhood of Manhattan songwriters.

10. twain—[C] two. Where the Mississippi River measured two fathoms in depth, steamship workers would call out, "Mark twain!" (hence the pen name of Samuel Clemens).

11. moxie—[B] courage. The word dates back to a soft drink in the 1800s.

12. brushback—[B] baseball pitch. It forces a batter to step back and breaks his confidence.

13. eighty-six—[B] get rid of. Rhyming with *nix*, it was originally diner slang meaning "to cancel."

14. copacetic—[A] very satisfactory. Its roots are unknown, but tap dancer Bill "Bojangles" Robinson claimed to have invented the word.

PICTURE THIS

Decals, a 19th-century invention, let people transfer pictures from paper to glass and other surfaces. Rumor is that by the early 1900s, fast-talking New Yorkers had jokily mashed the word *decalcomania* (the art of decal transfer) into *cockamamy*, slang for "nonsensical"—though etymologists aren't completely sure how!

TALKING POLITICS

Before you hit the polls, make sure you've mastered the lingo of the campaign trail. Try this quiz to see how politically correct your vocabulary is, then consult the next page for answers.

1. demagogue ('deh-meh-gog) *n.*—A: pollster. B: meeting. C: rabble-rouser.

2. plebiscite ('pleh-beh-siyt) *n.*—A: statement of loyalty. B: volunteer. C: countrywide vote.

3. chauvinist ('sho-veh-nist) *n.*—A: promoter of monarchy. B: political pundit. C: excessive patriot.

4. reactionary (ree-'ak-shuh-nary) *adj.*—A: very liberal. B: very conservative. C: undecided.

5. canvass ('kan-vas) *v.*—A: solicit voters. B: stretch a budget. C: attempt a cover-up.

6. hustings ('huhs-tingz) *n.*—A: nominee's supporters. B: proceedings or locale of a campaign. C: ballot punch-outs.

7. gravitas ('gra-veh-tahs) *n.*—A: perks and freebies. B: local leanings. C: serious bearing.

8. snollygoster ('snahlee-gahster) *n.*—A: unprincipled but shrewd person. B: loud argument. C: close vote.

9. incendiary (in-'sen-dee-er-ee) *adj.*—A: illegal. B: tending to excite or agitate. C: rising in power.

10. suffrage ('suh-frij) *n.*—A: right to vote. B: media exposure. C: civil disobedience.

11. jobbery ('jah-beh-ree) *n.*—A: works program. B: false persona. C: corruption in office.

12. éminence grise (ay-may-nahns 'greez) *n.*—A: confidential agent. B: diplomat. C: elite class.

13. laissez-faire ('le-'say-fair) *adj.*—A: proactive. B: opposing government interference. C: suave.

14. abdicate ('ab-di-kayt) *v.*—A: decline to vote. B: speak out of turn. C: resign from power.

15. junket ('juhn-ket) *n.*—A: government-paid trip. B: smear campaign. C: bad loan.

"Talking Politics" Answers

1. demagogue—[C] rabble-rouser. The senator's campaign turned ugly once the unofficial *demagogue* became manager.

2. plebiscite—[C] countrywide vote. We're having a *plebiscite* on whether countrywide votes are legitimate.

3. chauvinist—[C] excessive patriot. The governor is a true *chauvinist*: He wears Stars and Stripes boxers to bed. [The term, from purported 19th-century French nationalist Nicolas Chauvin, didn't take on the extremist "male chauvinist" meaning until the 1970s.]

4. reactionary—[B] very conservative. Larry is so *reactionary*, he won't even consider amending the education bill.

5. canvass—[A] solicit voters. Ever the all-American, Sally *canvassed* door-to-door toting a flag and an apple pie.

6. hustings—[B] proceedings or locale of a campaign. He doesn't really care if he wins; he just likes the bus rides to the various *hustings*.

7. gravitas—[C] serious bearing. How can you assume political *gravitas* with a name like Duckwill?

8. snollygoster—[A] unprincipled but shrewd person. There's something of a *snollygoster* in Governor Tooney's public persona.

9. incendiary—[B] tending to excite or agitate. My youngest girl is composing an *incendiary* speech about unionizing.

10. suffrage—[A] right to vote. So I told her, no, she doesn't have *suffrage* on matters of bedtime.

11. jobbery—[C] corruption in office. How is it *jobbery* if my friends just happened to all get on the payroll?

12. éminence grise—[A] confidential agent. It says Joey's Lemonade Stand, but Ella is the business's *éminence grise*.

13. laissez-faire—[B] opposing government interference. Joan seems to have a *laissez-faire* attitude about controlling her classroom.

14. abdicate—[C] resign from power. You can't depose me—I *abdicate*!

15. junket—[A] government-paid trip. I hear the boss went on a Busch Gardens *junket* using our pension fund!

HIP-HOP *HAMILTON*

The musical *Hamilton* by Lin-Manuel Miranda features a hip-hop libretto packed with rich vocabulary. Here are some words to know before seeing the historical show—if you can get a ticket! But there's no wait for the answers, which are on the next page, complete with lines from the Broadway smash.

1. manumission (man-yoo-'mih-shin) *n.*—A: spy operation. B: the act of freeing from slavery. C: handiwork.

2. complicit (kom-'plih-siht) *adj.*—A: elaborate. B: in total agreement. C: associating with or participating in.

3. equivocate (ih-'kwih-vuh-kayt) *v.*—A: waffle. B: share evenly. C: tremble.

4. enterprising ('ehn-ter-pry-zing) *adj.*—A: go-getting. B: trespassing. C: just beginning.

5. homilies ('hah-muh-leez) *n.*—A: family relations. B: sermons. C: opposites.

6. venerated ('veh-nuh-ray-ted) *adj.*—A: exhausted. B: honored. C: pardoned.

7. restitution (res-tih-'too-shuhn) *n.*—A: truce. B: imprisonment. C: amends.

8. dissidents ('diss-ih-dihnts) *n.*—A: dissenters. B: immigrants. C: tossers of insults.

9. obfuscates ('ahb-fuh-skayts) *v.*—A: substitutes. B: glides gracefully. C: confuses.

10. jettison ('jeh-tih-sen) *v.*—A: turn black. B: rise rapidly. C: throw away.

11. intemperate (ihn-'tem-puh-riht) *adj.*—A: permanent. B: hard to resist. C: unrestrained.

12. vacuous ('va-kew-uhs) *adj.*—A: empty or blank. B: gusting. C: immune.

13. intransigent (ihn-'tran-zih-jent) *adj.*—A: stubborn. B: revolting. C: on the move.

14. inimitable (ihn-'ih-mih-tuh-buhl) *adj.*—A: incomparable or unrivaled. B: undivided. C: countless.

15. disparage (di-'spar-ij) *v.*—A: scatter. B: speak ill of. C: fire, as cannons.

"Hip-Hop *Hamilton*" Answers

1. manumission—[B] the act of freeing from slavery. Alexander Hamilton: "[We are] a bunch of revolutionary *manumission* abolitionists."

2. complicit—[C] associating with or participating in. Thomas Jefferson: "I am *complicit* in watchin' him grabbin' at power and kiss it."

3. equivocate—[A] waffle. Hamilton: "I will not *equivocate* on my opinion."

4. enterprising—[A] go-getting. Jefferson: "These are wise words, *enterprising* men quote 'em."

5. homilies—[B] sermons. Aaron Burr: "These are things that the *homilies* and hymns won't teach ya."

6. venerated—[B] honored. George Washington: "I'm ... the *venerated* Virginian veteran."

7. restitution—[C] amends. Burr: "He woulda been dead or destitute without a cent or *restitution*."

8. dissidents—[A] dissenters.

Jefferson: "If Washington isn't gon' listen to disciplined *dissidents* ..."

9. obfuscates—[C] confuses. James Madison: "Ask him a question: It glances off, he *obfuscates*, he dances."

10. jettison—[C] throw away. Hamilton: "There isn't a plan he doesn't *jettison*."

11. intemperate—[C] unrestrained. Burr: "*Intemperate* indeed, good man."

12. vacuous—[A] empty or blank. Jefferson: "Gimme some dirt on this *vacuous* mass so we can at last unmask him."

13. intransigent—[A] stubborn. Hamilton: "These Virginians are ... being *intransigent*."

14. inimitable—[A] incomparable or unrivaled. Burr: "I am *inimitable*. I am an original."

15. disparage—[B] speak ill of. Philip Hamilton: "He *disparaged* my family's legacy in front of a crowd."

SHAPE SHIFTING

In the play, Alexander Hamilton is described as *protean*. This adjective comes to us from Proteus, a Greek sea god who could transform his shape at will—in Homer's *Odyssey*, Proteus transforms into a lion, a tree, and even running water. In human terms, it refers to someone who has great versatility or someone whose personality seems ever-changing. If you've had two or three wildly different careers, you might be called protean.

NATIVE AMERICAN ROOTS

Some Native American words adopted into English are as common as a backyard chipmunk (that's from the Ojibwa tribe), but there are plenty that are as unusual as a manatee in a mackinaw. For answers and etymology, turn to the next page.

1. mackinaw ('ma-kuh-naw) *n.*—
A: mountain creek. B: makeshift bed. C: wool coat.

2. dory ('dohr-ee) *n.*—A: dry gulch. B: flat-bottomed boat. C: small red potato.

3. hogan ('hoh-gahn) *n.*—
A: town meeting. B: log home. C: ceremonial pipe.

4. punkie ('puhn-kee) *n.*—
A: wooden sled. B: biting bug. C: runt of a litter.

5. dowitcher ('dow-ih-chur) *n.*—
A: wading bird. B: widow. C: gifted healer.

6. Podunk ('poh-dunk) *n.*—
A: small town. B: swimming hole. C: fried cake.

7. manatee ('ma-nuh-tee) *n.*—
A: carved face. B: sea cow. C: hard-fought contest.

8. pogonip ('pah-guh-nihp) *n.*—
A: ball game. B: organic snack. C: cold fog.

9. potlatch ('paht-lach) *n.*—
A: straw hat. B: red pigment. C: celebratory feast.

10. kachina (kuh-'chee-nuh) *n.*—
A: rain shower. B: wooden doll. C: drum.

11. savanna (suh-'va-nuh) *n.*—
A: voyage on foot. B: expression of adoration. C: grassland.

12. terrapin ('tehr-uh-pin) *n.*—
A: spring flower. B: swampland. C: turtle.

13. hackmatack ('hak-muh-tak) *n.*—A: larch tree. B: machete. C: ambush.

14. sachem ('say-chum) *n.*—
A: hex or curse. B: puff of smoke. C: leader.

15. chinook (shih-'nook) *n.*—
A: convicted thief. B: warm wind. C: campfire.

"Native American Roots" Answers

1. mackinaw—[C] wool coat. Joseph always wears his *mackinaw*, even on warm, sunny days. (Algonquian)

2. dory—[B] flat-bottomed boat. Susan's favorite way to relax is fishing from her *dory* on the bay. (Miskito)

3. hogan—[B] log home. The doorway of a traditional *hogan* faces east, toward the sunrise. (Navajo)

4. punkie—[B] biting bug. Whether you call them midges, no-see-ums, or *punkies*, they're all out for blood! (Delaware)

5. dowitcher—[A] wading bird. According to my field guide, that bird is a long-billed *dowitcher*. (Iroquois)

6. Podunk—[A] small town. Who could have imagined that this kid from *Podunk* would make it big? (Algonquian)

7. manatee—[B] sea cow. *Manatees* use their flippers to "walk" along the seabed while grazing on plants. (Cariban)

8. pogonip—[C] cold fog. Thanks to this morning's *pogonip*, I have ice crystals in my eyebrows. (Shoshone)

9. potlatch—[C] celebratory feast. Geno's mac and cheese is a favorite at his family's annual *potlatch*. (Nootka)

10. kachina—[B] wooden doll. The museum has an impressive collection of hand-carved *kachinas*. (Hopi)

11. savanna—[C] grassland. On his tour of African *savannas*, Eli spotted elephants, zebras, and rhinos. (Taino)

12. terrapin—[C] turtle. On summer days, *terrapins* sun themselves on flat rocks in the marsh. (Algonquian)

13. hackmatack—[A] larch tree. Will you have a picnic under the *hackmatack* with me? (Algonquian)

14. sachem—[C] leader. The CEO may sit in the corner office, but in this company the marketing director is the real *sachem*. (Narragansett)

15. chinook—[B] warm wind. The *chinook* blew in from the southwest, melting the last of the winter snow. (Chehalis)

SAY THAT AGAIN?

We can thank the Nipmuc people of Massachusetts for the longest place name in America. With 45 letters and 14 syllables, Lake Chargoggagoggmanchauggagoggchaubunagungamaugg certainly presents a challenge to sign painters. Fortunately, it's also known by a shorter (and more pronounceable) name: Webster Lake.

GIVING THANKS

Add some zest to your vocabulary with this feast of nutritious words and phrases, perfect for Thanksgiving—or any time you're hungry. If you can't stand the heat in our kitchen, cool off with the answers on the next page.

1. gustatory ('guh-stuh-tohr-ee) *adj.*—A: full-bellied. B: relating to taste. C: rich and flavorful.

2. au gratin (oh 'grah-tin) *adj.*— A: cooked to medium rare. B: free of charge. C: covered with cheese and browned.

3. succulent ('suh-kyu-lent) *adj.*— A: sun-dried. B: juicy. C: sipped with a straw.

4. mesclun ('mess-klen) *n.*— A: mix of greens. B: shellfish. C: Cajun dipping sauce.

5. piquant ('pee-kent) *adj.*— A: in season. B: in small amounts. C: spicy.

6. chiffonade (shih-fuh-'nayd) *n.*— A: whipped margarine. B: shredded herbs or veggies. C: lemon pudding.

7. toothsome ('tooth-sum) *adj.*— A: chewy. B: delicious. C: hungry.

8. sous vide (soo 'veed) *adv.*— A: without salt. B: on the side. C: cooked in a pouch.

9. culinary ('kuh-lih-nehr-ee) *adj.*—A: of the kitchen. B: buttery. C: cage-free.

10. umami (ooh-'mah-mee) *n.*— A: oven rack. B: chopsticks. C: savory taste.

11. tempeh ('tem-pay) *n.*—A: part-time chef. B: soy cake. C: fondue pot.

12. fricassee ('frih-kuh-see) *v.*— A: cut and stew in gravy. B: deep-fry. C: sauté with mushrooms.

13. oenophile ('ee-nuh-fiyl) *n.*— A: wine lover. B: food critic. C: egg fancier.

14. poach (pohch) *v.*— A: cook in simmering liquid. B: fry in a small amount of fat. C: heat slowly in a covered pot.

15. fondant ('fahn-duhnt) *n.*— A: food lover. B: cake icing. C: large bib.

"Giving Thanks" Answers

1. gustatory—[B] relating to taste. Here, try my new *gustatory* experiment—beet ice cream!

2. au gratin—[C] covered with cheese and browned. Is there anything better than onion soup *au gratin* on a cold, rainy day?

3. succulent—[B] juicy. For dessert, the chef served pound cake topped with *succulent* pears.

4. mesclun—[A] mix of greens. "You call this a salad? It's just a plate of wilted *mesclun*."

5. piquant—[C] spicy. The *piquant* smells from the Mexican restaurant wafted out onto the street.

6. chiffonade—[B] shredded herbs or veggies. If you add a *chiffonade* of fresh basil, this frozen pizza isn't half bad!

7. toothsome—[B] delicious. Hattie makes the most *toothsome* cherry pie I've ever tasted.

8. sous vide—[C] cooked in a pouch. Though preparing steak *sous vide* takes time, it will cook your meat evenly and retain the moisture.

9. culinary—[A] of the kitchen. Julia Child was a true *culinary* icon.

10. umami—[C] savory taste. *Umami* is one of the five basic tastes, along with sweet, sour, salty, and bitter.

11. tempeh—[B] soy cake. Ezra, a devoted vegan, serves *tempeh* burgers and tofu dogs at his cookouts.

12. fricassee—[A] cut and stew in gravy. Tired of turkey sandwiches and turkey soup, Hector decided to *fricassee* the leftovers from his Thanksgiving bird.

13. oenophile—[A] wine lover. A serious *oenophile*, Adrienne was horrified when her date added ice cubes to his pinot noir.

14. poach—[A] cook in simmering liquid. For breakfast, Sasha loves to *poach* an egg and pair it with avocado toast topped with tomato.

15. fondant—[B] cake icing. Kelly flunked her cake-making class when she slathered on too much *fondant*.

WHAT KIND OF FOOD PERSON ARE YOU?

If you appreciate fine dining, you might call yourself a *gourmet*, an *epicure*, or a *bon vivant*. If you have a healthy but unrefined appetite, you're a *gourmand* or a *trencherman*. And if you've done your homework on the history and rituals of haute cuisine, you're a *gastronome* (*gastronomy* is the art or science of good eating).

IDEAS & IDEALS

It's one thing to feel that you are on the right path,
but it's another to think that yours is the only path.
—PAULO COELHO

"

Injustice anywhere is a threat to justice everywhere.
—REV. MARTIN LUTHER KING JR.

"

A bookstore is one of the only pieces of evidence
we have that people are still thinking.
—JERRY SEINFELD

"

Curious learning not only makes unpleasant
things less unpleasant but also makes pleasant
things more pleasant.
—BERTRAND RUSSELL

"

When a generation talks just to itself, it becomes
more filled with folly than it might have otherwise.
—STEWART BRAND

"

I think everybody has a right to happiness
and freedom and security and health care
and education and guitar lessons.
—BONNIE RAITT

THE PERFECT WORDS FOR
OPEN COURT

A great many people in this country are worried
about law-and-order. And a great many people are
worried about justice. But one thing is certain:
you cannot have either until you have both.
—RAMSEY CLARK

"
Justice is the insurance we have on our lives,
and obedience is the premium we pay for it.
—WILLIAM PENN

"
Injustice is relatively easy to bear;
what stings is justice.
—H. L. MENCKEN

"
The worst form of injustice
is pretended justice.
—PLATO

That old law about "an eye for an eye"
leaves everybody blind.
—REV. MARTIN LUTHER KING JR.

In matters of truth and justice, there is no difference between large and small problems, for issues concerning the treatment of people are all the same.

—ALBERT EINSTEIN

"

It's every man's business to see justice done.

—SIR ARTHUR CONAN DOYLE

"

I would uphold the law if for no other reason but to protect myself.

—THOMAS MORE

"

It is better to risk saving a guilty man than to condemn an innocent one.

—VOLTAIRE

"

Injustice alone can shake down the pillars of the skies, and restore the reign of Chaos and Night.

—HORACE MANN

"

Defending the truth is not something one does out of a sense of duty or to allay guilt complexes, but is a reward in itself.

—SIMONE DE BEAUVOIR

> I am simple, complex, generous, selfish, unattractive, beautiful, lazy, and driven.
>
> **—BARBRA STREISAND**

AGING GRACEFULLY

The older we get, the more we learn about the world—or so we hope. It may not be fun to watch our faces and bodies change over the years, but the life lessons we've learned are reflected back at us each time we look in the mirror.

LOVE THE ONE YOU'RE WITH

Be happy in your body. . . . It's the only one
you've got, so you might as well like it.
—KEIRA KNIGHTLEY

"

I really don't think I need buns of steel.
I'd be happy with buns of cinnamon.
—ELLEN DEGENERES

"

I'm not overweight. I'm just nine inches too short.
—SHELLEY WINTERS

"

If you want to look young and thin,
hang around old fat people.
—JIM EASON

"

I'd rather be a few pounds heavier and enjoy
life than be worried all the time.
—DREW BARRYMORE

"

Even the worst haircut eventually grows out.
—LISA KOGAN

Happiness is the best facelift.
—DIANA KRALL

"

Beauty, to me, is about being comfortable in your own skin. That, or a kick-ass red lipstick.
—GWYNETH PALTROW

"

I would rather be called funny than pretty.
—NIA VARDALOS

"

The most beautiful makeup for a woman is passion. But cosmetics are easier to buy.
—YVES ST. LAURENT

"

It seems with every match I win, I get better-looking to other people.
—ANDY RODDICK

"

It's great to be a blonde. With low expectations it's very easy to surprise people.
—PAMELA ANDERSON

🐦 QUOTABLE TWEETS

It's all about lovin' not only who we see in the mirror, but what we feel about ourselves when we look in the mirror.

@TYRABANKS

WORKING IT OUT

I don't exercise. If God had wanted me to bend over,
he would have put diamonds on the floor.

—JOAN RIVERS

"

The word *aerobics* came about when the gym instructors
got together and said, "If we're going to charge
$10 an hour, we can't call it jumping up and down."

—RITA RUDNER

"

I'm so unfamiliar with the gym I call it James.

—CHI MCBRIDE

"

It's all right letting yourself go, as long as you can get
yourself back.

—MICK JAGGER

"

I decided I can't pay a person to rewind time,
so I may as well get over it.

—SERENA WILLIAMS

 QUOTABLE TWEETS

People always ask me: "WHY?! OH GOD
WHY?!!?" Mostly at the beach.

@CONANOBRIEN

TO YOUR HEALTH

The first wealth is health.
—RALPH WALDO EMERSON

"

The best beauty secret is sunblock.
—CHRISTIE BRINKLEY

"

Eat right, exercise regularly, die anyway.
—UNKNOWN

"

God gave us the gift of life; it is up to us
to give ourselves the gift of living well.
—VOLTAIRE

"

I believe that how you feel is very important to
how you look—that healthy equals beautiful.
—VICTORIA PRINCIPAL

AGING WELL

You can get old pretty young if you
don't take care of yourself.

—YOGI BERRA

"

The ball doesn't know how old I am.

—MARTINA NAVRATILOVA

"

I don't want to get to the end of my life and find
that I have lived just the length of it. I want
to have lived the width of it as well.

—DIANE ACKERMAN

"

Forget aging. If you're six feet above ground,
it's a good day.

—FAITH HILL

🐦 **QUOTABLE TWEETS**

Happy Birthday, Thomas Hayward.
Unfortunately he's dead, he would
have been 177 today. Only a year
younger than me…

@JOHNCLEESE

The only thing that has ever made me feel old is those few times where I allow myself to be predictable.
—CARLOS SANTANA

"

The heart ages last.
—SYLVESTER STALLONE

"

Maturity is a high price to pay for growing up.
—TOM STOPPARD

"

I don't feel old. I don't feel anything till noon. That's when it's time for my nap.
—BOB HOPE

"

One day I woke up and I was the oldest person in every room.
—BILL CLINTON

"

Life asks us to make measurable progress in reasonable time. That's why they make those fourth-grade chairs so small—so you won't fit in them at age 25.
—JIM ROHN

"

The older I get, the better I used to be.
—JOHN MCENROE

GET-WELL CARDS

I wonder why you can always read a doctor's bill
and you can never read his prescription.

—FINLEY PETER DUNNE

"

If you're going through hell, keep going.

—WINSTON CHURCHILL

"

Sleep, riches, and health to be truly
enjoyed must be interrupted.

—JOHANN PAUL FRIEDRICH RICHTER

"

When you come to the end of your rope,
tie a knot and hang on.

—FRANKLIN D. ROOSEVELT

"

To array a man's will against his sickness
is the supreme art of medicine.

—HENRY WARD BEECHER

"

Sickness comes on horseback but departs on foot.

—DUTCH PROVERB

FAMOUS WORDS

The words in this quiz come from the book *Favorite Words of Famous People* by Lewis Burke Frumkes. Turn the page for answers—and to see which notable names picked these terms for top billing.

1. plangent ('plan-jent) *adj.*— A: flexible. B: very loud. C: carefully detailed.

2. ruckus ('ruh-kuhs) *n.*— A: backpack. B: melee. C: dry gully.

3. vermilion (ver-'mil-yun) *n.*—A: ten-figure number. B: moth larva. C: bright red.

4. chthonic ('thah-nik) *adj.*— A: of the underworld. B: frozen solid. C: having sharp claws.

5. gormless ('gorm-les) *adj.*—A: nonflowering. B: lacking firm shape. C: stupid.

6. interstitial (ihn-ter-'stih-shuhl) *adj.*—A: beyond our solar system. B: in the spaces between. C: joined by stitches.

7. unilateral (yoo-nih-'la-tuh-ruhl) *adj.*—A: one-sided. B: in alliance with. C: flat.

8. palimpsest ('pa-lehmp-sehst) *n.*—A: spotted pony. B: leg brace. C: written-over document.

9. beguiling (bih-'guy-ling) *adj.*—A: twisted together. B: complementary. C: cleverly deceptive.

10. lambent ('lam-buhnt) *adj.*— A: easily dissolved. B: submissive. C: luminous.

11. incarnadine (ihn-'kar-nuh-dine) *adj.*—A: flesh-colored. B: reborn. C: not digestible.

12. phosphorescent (fos-fuh-'reh-sent) *adj.*—A: of ocean depths. B: glittering. C: soapy.

13. ramshackle ('ram-sha-kuhl) *adj.*—A: barnlike. B: rickety-looking. C: falsely imprisoned.

14. pixilated (pick-suh-'lay-ted) *adj.*—A: grainy or blurry. B: elfin. C: mentally unbalanced.

15. qua ('kwah) *prep.*—A: in the capacity of. B: starting from. C: in the immediate neighborhood of.

"Famous Words" Answers

1. plangent—[B] very loud. My nephew blasts *plangent*, sad music in his room. (director Wes Craven)

2. ruckus—[B] melee. There was quite a *ruckus* when the fire alarm went off. (Penn Jillette of Penn & Teller)

3. vermilion—[C] bright red. The theater had eye-catching *vermilion* walls. (writer A. S. Byatt)

4. chthonic—[A] of the underworld. I love the story of Orpheus's *chthonic* journey. (Margaret Atwood)

5. gormless—[C] stupid. The writer dismissed his critics as *gormless* twits. (author Barbara Taylor Bradford)

6. interstitial—[B] in the spaces between. The film's action sequences were thrilling; I found the *interstitial* scenes rather dull. (Al Gore)

7. unilateral—[A] one-sided. The volleyball squad had a *unilateral* advantage in height. (editor Helen Gurley Brown)

8. palimpsest—[C] written-over document. My address book is a *palimpsest*—I keep erasing names and adding new ones. (Joyce Carol Oates)

9. beguiling—[C] cleverly deceptive. Those *beguiling* ads persuaded me to buy a phone I didn't really need. (playwright Wendy Wasserstein)

10. lambent—[C] luminous. Sofia loved hiking by the *lambent* moonlight. (activist Andrea Dworkin)

11. incarnadine—[A] flesh-colored. Mia chose a pretty *incarnadine* dress for the wedding. (Arthur C. Clarke)

12. phosphorescent—[B] glittering. The *phosphorescent* firefly flew right into the jar. (John Updike)

13. ramshackle—[B] rickety-looking. Jack carefully stepped onto the *ramshackle* bridge. (Ray Bradbury)

14. pixilated—[C] mentally unbalanced. Dad's *pixilated* behavior has us worried. (Mark Hamill)

15. qua—[A] in the capacity of. Forget the painter's political views—can we enjoy her art *qua* art? (Dave Barry)

OTHER FAVORITES

Crime writer Edna Buchanan liked *berserk* ("crazed") and *amok* ("in a murderously frenzied state") best. Actor and dancer Gene Kelly chose *plethora* ("excess"). Comedian Bob Hope went with *laughter*, while journalist Dan Rather selected *courage*. And TV host Larry King singled out *why*, saying, "It's the best word in the universe. Think about it."

SHARP DRESSER

This time, we challenge your fashion sense—that is, your knowledge of words about clothing and style. Fit to be tied? Turn the page for answers.

1. décolletage (day-kah-le-'tazh) *n.*—A: low-cut neckline. B: school uniform. C: clothing sale.

2. sartorial (sar-'tor-ee-ul) *adj.*— A: relating to a tailor or tailored clothes. B: relating to shoes. C: made out of wool.

3. ruched ('roosht) *adj.*—A: tied in a bow. B: pleated or bunched. C: dyed blue.

4. argyle ('ar-giyl) *adj.*—A: in pinstripes. B: in diamond patterns. C: polka-dotted.

5. twee ('twee) *adj.*—A: spotted with stains. B: having a veil over the face. C: excessively dainty or cute.

6. salopettes ('sal-eh-pets) *n.*— A: wooden shoes. B: skier's overalls. C: cuff links.

7. caparison (ke-'per-uh-sun) *n.*— A: selection of hats. B: ornamental covering for a horse. C: jester's costume.

8. bouffant (boo-'fahnt or 'boo-fahnt) *adj.*—A: flowery. B: puffed-out. C: skin-tight.

9. ikat ('ee-kaht) *n.*—A: head scarf. B: shoelace tip. C: tie-dyed fabric.

10. bespoke (bih-'spohk) *adj.*— A: custom-made. B: color-coordinated. C: with circular designs.

11. clew ('klew) *n.*—A: ball of yarn. B: run in a stocking. C: alligator skin.

12. regalia (ri-'gayl-yeh) *n.*— A: everyday wear. B: magnificent attire. C: lingerie.

13. panache (puh-'nash or -'nahsh) *n.*—A: handkerchief. B: untucked shirttail. C: flamboyance in style.

14. prink ('prink) *v.*—A: perforate. B: dress carefully. C: go down one size.

15. sporran ('spor-en) *n.*—A: lobster bib. B: pouch worn with a kilt. C: ruffed collar or sleeve.

"Sharp Dresser" Answers

1. décolletage—[A] low-cut neckline. A stray rolling pea disappeared down Lady Buxton's *décolletage*.

2. sartorial—[A] relating to a tailor or tailored clothes. If you had any *sartorial* respect, you wouldn't dunk my Burberry jacket sleeve in gravy.

3. ruched—[B] pleated or bunched. Taking a trend too far, Lucy had *ruched* tablecloths, curtains, and slipcovers.

4. argyle—[B] in diamond patterns. Roy found that his *argyle* socks worked well as meatball catapults.

5. twee—[C] excessively dainty or cute. That pink dress might suit you, but isn't it a bit *twee* for the barbecue?

6. salopettes—[B] skier's overalls. Carl's *salopettes* may have stood out on the slope, but they did nothing to enhance his downhill performance.

7. caparison—[B] ornamental covering for a horse. The "medieval" battle looked authentic to us, right down to the *caparisons* for the horses.

8. bouffant—[B] puffed-out. The gown's *bouffant* skirt was the perfect complement to the bride's hairdo.

9. ikat—[C] tie-dyed fabric. In head-to-toe *ikat*, Rufus looked rather psychedelic.

10. bespoke—[A] custom-made. Lyle enjoyed showing off his *bespoke* ten-gallon hat at dinner last night.

11. clew—[A] ball of yarn. Follow this unraveled *clew* far enough, and you'll find Casper, my tabby kitten.

12. regalia—[B] magnificent attire. Eva's *regalia* sure made a statement at last night's state dinner.

13. panache—[C] flamboyance in style. Yes, Charlie leads an exciting, outrageous life, but he doesn't quite have the *panache* of a Hollywood playboy.

14. prink—[B] dress carefully. Lauren *prinks* for hours before each date.

15. sporran—[B] pouch worn with a kilt. Rushing out the door for the parade, my brother shouted, "Has anyone seen my *sporran*?"

NEWSWORTHY

Each week, the folks at merriam-webster.com highlight a word that's in the news. Here's a sampling from their Trend Watch section from May 2015. Check the next page for answers.

1. amnesty ('am-neh-stee) *n.*—
A: treason. B: pardon. C: safe haven.

2. harridan ('har-eh-den) *n.*—
A: brief, wild storm. B: mercenary soldier. C: haggard, old woman.

3. repudiate (rih-'pyu-dee-ayt) *v.*—A: overthrow. B: refuse to accept or support. C: divulge.

4. indict (en-'diyt) *v.*—A: point out. B: charge with a crime. C: vote.

5. gentrification (jen-treh-feh-'kay-shehn) *n.*—A: gender switch. B: uncultured upbringing. C: displacement of the poor by the affluent.

6. sovereignty ('sahv-er-en-tee) *n.*—A: full knowledge. B: supreme power. C: communal state.

7. conflate (kon-'flayt) *v.*—A: barter or deal. B: ignore. C: confuse or combine into a whole.

8. solipsistic (soh-lep-'sis-tik) *adj.*—A: highly egocentric. B: slick. C: applied to the lips.

9. intransigence (in-'tran-sih-jents) *n.*—A: stubbornness. B: hard travel. C: secret information.

10. subterfuge ('sub-ter-fyewj) *n.*—A: deceptive stratagem. B: underwater dwelling. C: cheap replica.

11. inherent (in-'hir-ent) *adj.*—A: inborn. B: granted by a will. C: leased for low cost.

12. eponymous (ih-'pah-neh-mes) *adj.*—A: unsigned. B: opposite in meaning. C: named for a person.

13. intrepid (in-'treh-pid) *adj.*—A: stumbling. B: unpleasantly hot. C: fearless.

14. sectarian (sek-'ter-ee-an) *adj.*—A: related to a horse. B: of religious factions. C: having six parts.

15. culpable ('kuhl-peh-buhl) *adj.*—A: blameworthy. B: likely to happen. C: not competent.

"Newsworthy" Answers

1. amnesty—[B] pardon. President Obama's deportation *amnesty* is a key controversy across the nation.

2. harridan—[C] haggard, old woman. During trial, former Virginia governor Bob McDonnell portrayed his wife as a *harridan*, said the *New York Times*.

3. repudiate—[B] refuse to accept or support. After the midterm elections, Senator Paul said, "Tonight is a *repudiation* of Barack Obama's policies."

4. indict—[B] charge with a crime. Darren Wilson was not *indicted* for the killing of Michael Brown.

5. gentrification—[C] displacement of the poor by the affluent. Spike Lee has denounced the *gentrification* in neighborhoods such as Fort Greene.

6. sovereignty—[B] supreme power. Ukraine will not settle its conflicts with Russia until it regains full *sovereignty* over Crimea.

7. conflate—[C] confuse or combine into a whole. Newsman Brian Williams doesn't know what caused him to "*conflate* one aircraft with another."

8. solipsistic—[A] highly egocentric. Some view Facebook as a simply *solipsistic* forum.

9. intransigence—[A] stubbornness. The government shutdown was a display of *intransigence*, said the *Los Angeles Times*.

10. subterfuge—[A] deceptive stratagem. Democratic leader Nancy Pelosi said the Republicans' intent to sue the president was a "*subterfuge*."

11. inherent—[A] inborn. When the Declaration of Independence refers to "unalienable" rights, it is describing the *inherent* privileges people are entitled to.

12. eponymous—[C] named for a person. Who was the original Oscar behind the *eponymous* statuette?

13. intrepid—[C] fearless. After "stealing" a block while playing, Prince George was called "very *intrepid*."

14. sectarian—[B] of religious factions. The UN has warned of "further *sectarian* violence" in Iraq.

15. culpable—[A] blameworthy. Oscar Pistorius was found guilty of *culpable* homicide in South Africa.

WHY WE CAST ABOUT
The word *cast* has its roots in Middle English via the Old Norse *kasta*, meaning "to throw." This is close to the modern definition of "to put forth." So it makes sense that now a newscaster can broadcast the forecast.

BODY LANGUAGE

When the ancient Greeks inscribed the phrase "Know thyself" at the temple of Apollo, we're pretty sure they meant it in the philosophical sense. But how well do you know thyself in a physical sense? This month's quiz tests your knowledge of words related to the body. Can't put your finger on a definition? See the next page for answers.

1. mental *adj.*—of or relating to… A: the navel. B: the chin. C: the hands or feet.

2. visage *n.*—A: face. B: lens of the eye. C: type of birthmark.

3. hirsute *adj.*—A: bent over with hands on knees. B: barrel-chested. C: hairy.

4. pectoral *adj.*—A: of the side. B: of the back. C: of the chest.

5. corpulent *adj.*—A: of or relating to the skull. B: bulky or stout. C: frail, as a bone.

6. alopecia *n.*—A: skin reddening. B: baldness. C: mythological beauty.

7. nuque *n.*—A: back of the neck. B: arch of the foot. C: tip of the tongue.

8. hemic *adj.*—A: of the liver. B: of the blood. C: of the stomach.

9. gangling *adj.*—A: infected. B: bunched, as nerves. C: awkwardly tall and thin.

10. cerumen *n.*—A: type of leg brace. B: essential protein. C: earwax.

11. pollex *n.*—A: kneecap or the tissue surrounding it. B: thumb. C: bridge between the nostrils.

12. ventral *adj.*—A: around the stomach. B: leaving the body, as exhaled air. C: fully developed, as a muscle.

13. axilla *n.*—A: network of nerves along the spine. B: long bone of the leg. C: armpit.

14. ossicles *n.*—A: small bones in the ear. B: nerves attached to the eye. C: eyelashes.

15. fontanel *n.*—A: bone in the finger. B: lower-back muscle. C: soft spot in a young skull.

"Body Language" Answers

1. mental—[B] of or relating to the chin. The boxing vet gave the cocky kid a little *mental* reminder halfway through the first round.

2. visage—[A] face. Harlan stared hard at the *visage* in the painting, curious about its smile.

3. hirsute—[C] hairy. "That's a great costume," Alan admitted. "But you're missing the *hirsute* hobbit feet."

4. pectoral—[C] of the chest. The weight lifter flexed his *pectoral* muscles in a truly Hulkian spectacle.

5. corpulent—[B] bulky or stout. Tara wouldn't call her brother overweight, just a little *corpulent*.

6. alopecia—[B] baldness. Art has been shaving his head since he was 21, hoping to hide his *alopecia*.

7. nuque—[A] back of the neck. Grazing Mary's *nuque*, Hugo thought, was a subtle sign of affection. She disagreed.

8. hemic—[B] of the blood. Would it be fair to say the *Twilight* characters have a slight *hemic* obsession?

9. gangling—[C] awkwardly tall and thin. The new teacher was a *gangling* figure from Sleepy Hollow, best known for another spindly pedagogue, Ichabod Crane.

10. cerumen—[C] earwax. "I certainly doubt *cerumen* is keeping you from hearing me," the instructor barked, glaring at her student's headphones.

11. pollex—[B] thumb. "That's a thimble," Gracie explained to her granddaughter during their sewing lesson. "It's the best way to protect your *pollex*."

12. ventral—[A] around the stomach. His *ventral* fat, the *Biggest Loser* contestant hoped, would be the first to go.

13. axilla—[C] armpit. The second grader's favorite gag involved his cupped hand and his *axilla*.

14. ossicles—[A] small bones in the ear. "For extra credit, what are the smallest bones in the human body?" Mr. Griffin asked. "The *ossicles*!" Tad shouted out.

15. fontanel—[C] soft spot in a young skull. "Mind his *fontanel*," the new mom said, handing her son to his nervous father.

MEASURING UP

We're counting on you to figure out these useful words about numbers, amounts, and measurements. Having trouble putting two and two together? Turn the page for answers.

1. fourscore ('fohr-skohr) *adj.*— A: sixteen. B: forty. C: eighty.

2. tabulate ('ta-byuh-layt) *v.*— A: rank by weight and height. B: count or arrange systematically. C: indent a column.

3. copious ('coh-pee-uhss) *adj.*— A: plentiful. B: scanty. C: carefully reproduced.

4. gross (grohss) *n.*—A: twelve dozen. B: 51 percent. C: two bushels.

5. aggregate ('a-grih-get) *adj.*— A: increasing exponentially. B: amounting to a whole. C: left over as a fraction.

6. googol ('goo-gaul) *n.*— A: negative number. B: value of pi. C: 1 followed by 100 zeros.

7. paucity ('paw-sih-tee) *n.*— A: overabundance. B: shortage. C: average.

8. myriad ('meer-ee-uhd) *adj.*— A: very heavy. B: immeasurably small. C: countless.

9. troika ('troy-kuh) *n.*— A: numbered wheel. B: group of three. C: ancient calculator.

10. calibrate ('ka-luh-brayt) *v.*— A: adjust according to a standard. B: divide into equal parts. C: gain heat.

11. manifold ('man-uh-fold) *adj.*—A: diverse. B: dwindling. C: doubled.

12. quota ('kwoh-tuh) *n.*— A: estimated profit. B: bottom line. C: preset percentage.

13. brace (brayss) *n.*—A: pair. B: trio. C: quartet.

14. cipher ('sy-fer) *n.*— A: zero. B: exponent. C: equal proportion.

15. cubed (kyoobd) *adj.*— A: tripled. B: cut into thirds. C: multiplied by itself twice.

"Measuring Up" Answers

1. fourscore—[C] eighty. That's the strangest thing I've heard in all my *fourscore* years.

2. tabulate—[B] count or arrange systematically. The committee has *tabulated* the votes—and determined that it's a tie!

3. copious—[A] plentiful. Harriet's notes from history class are *copious* but completely illegible.

4. gross—[A] twelve dozen. How many *gross* of cupcakes did you order for the Halloween party?

5. aggregate—[B] amounting to a whole. Analysts are expecting the *aggregate* demand for electric cars to skyrocket.

6. googol—[C] 1 followed by 100 zeros. Emile's chances of dating Jacqueline are about one in a *googol*.

7. paucity—[B] shortage. Given the *paucity* of evidence against the murder suspect, the detective reluctantly let her go.

8. myriad—[C] countless. Brooke plans to consume *myriad* pumpkin-spice-flavored products this fall.

9. troika—[B] group of three. In my opinion, Larry, Curly, and Moe are a *troika* of numbskulls.

10. calibrate—[A] adjust according to a standard. The post office *calibrates* its scale each morning before opening for business.

11. manifold—[A] diverse. There are *manifold* reasons why Cory's time machine experiment failed.

12. quota—[C] preset percentage. Are you saying one lousy cookie is my *quota* from this jar?

13. brace—[A] pair. We just adopted a *brace* of puppies, so it's kind of crazy around our house.

14. cipher—[A] zero. If you felt like a *cipher* in middle school, join the club!

15. cubed—[C] multiplied by itself twice. Three *cubed* is 27, the last time I checked.

THE NAME IS DEEP

When the young writer Samuel Clemens worked as a Mississippi riverboat pilot, he surely saw crewmen *sounding* the river—measuring its depth—with the call "Mark twain!" This meant they had measured two *fathoms*; a single fathom is six feet, and *twain* means "two." Clemens first used the byline Mark Twain in 1863, as a Nevada newspaper reporter.

WORDS OF YESTERYEAR

Language, colorful and complex, is always evolving. Some words are rooted in their time; others are merely useful for a time. This group is probably well known to grandparents if not to today's whippersnappers. How many do you know? Answers on next page.

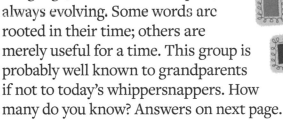

1. cordial—A: garden party. B: fruit-flavored liqueur. C: flower for buttonhole.

2. gumption—A: foolhardiness. B: resourcefulness. C: stickiness.

3. ragamuffin—A: child in dirty clothes. B: pie made with fruit and stale crumbs. C: abandoned house pet.

4. jalopy—A: beat-up car. B: vacant building. C: elderly gentleman.

5. ewer—A: wide-mouthed water jug. B: hand-crank pump. C: paddock for sheep.

6. lollygag—A: play a trick on someone. B: wolf down food. C: dawdle.

7. bustle—A: padding at the rear of a woman's skirt. B: undergarment used to constrict the waist. C: strapless bodice.

8. rapscallion—A: bitter vegetable. B: mischievous person. C: musical style.

9. gumshoe—A: detective. B: burglar. C: athlete.

10. gitches—A: arguments. B: underwear. C: silly people.

11. apothecary—A: fortune teller. B: pharmacist. C: evangelical minister.

12. balderdash—A: slang. B: exaggeration. C: nonsense.

13. dickey—A: chest pocket on overalls. B: false shirtfront. C: high-necked cape.

14. providence—A: happy coincidence. B: physical comfort. C: divine care.

15. naughty-naught—A: badly behaved child. B: girl's tangled hair. C: the year 1900.

16. pedal pushers—A: bicycle gears. B: calf-length trousers. C: two-tone shoes.

17. humdinger—A: laughable. B: modern. C: someone or something extraordinary.

"Words of Yesteryear" Answers

1. cordial—[B] fruit-flavored liqueur. Only favored guests were offered Aunt Millie's homemade raspberry *cordial*.

2. gumption—[B] resourcefulness. The Wright brothers sure had *gumption* to make and fly their planes.

3. ragamuffin—[A] child in dirty clothes. After picking up Arnie from the petting zoo, Grandma proclaimed, "He looks like the *ragamuffin* Oliver Twist!"

4. jalopy—[A] beat-up car. A constant eyesore, our neighbor's *jalopy* is ready for the junkyard.

5. ewer—[A] widemouthed water jug. A basin and *ewer* predate the modern bathroom sink.

6. lollygag—[C] dawdle. Don't *lollygag* on the way to school or you'll be late.

7. bustle—[A] padding at the rear of a woman's skirt. The *bustle* added some unneeded curves to her profile.

8. rapscallion—[B] mischievous person. That *rapscallion* tricked everyone into doing all his chores for him.

9. gumshoe—[A] detective. Who is your favorite *gumshoe*, Philip Marlowe or Sam Spade?

10. gitches—[B] underwear. It was so warm outside that little Sammy stripped down to his *gitches*.

11. apothecary—[B] pharmacist. Check with the *apothecary* about side effects before taking that drug.

12. balderdash—[C] nonsense. In response to vehement claims that the earth is flat, Galileo would always yell, "What *balderdash*!"

13. dickey—[B] false shirtfront. My great-uncle wore a *dickey*, saving my great-aunt from heaps of shirt washing.

14. providence—[C] divine care. Trusting in *providence*, Lillie booked a transatlantic voyage during hurricane season.

15. naughty-naught—[C] the year 1900. *Naughty-naught* cleverly hints at a daring new generation.

16. pedal pushers—[B] calf-length trousers. The costume designer had her hands full making *pedal pushers* for the play's revival.

17. humdinger—[C] something or someone extraordinary. That was a real *humdinger* of a storm last night.

VERBAL MISUSE AND ABUSE

Combat conversation miscues with our quiz—
which tackles some too-frequent examples
of verbal misuse (and abuse!). How sure are you
about these troublemaking morphemes?
Answers on next page.

1. noisome ('noy-sum) *adj.*—
A: loud. B: stinky. C: crowded.

2. enervated ('eh-ner-vayt-ed)
adj.—A: lacking energy. B: refreshed.
C: feeling anxiety.

3. proscribe (proh-'skriyb) *v.*—
A: encourage. B: dispense a medicine.
C: forbid.

4. nonplussed (non-'pluhst)
adj.—A: baffled. B: cool under
pressure. C: subtracted.

5. principle ('prin-seh-pul) *n.*—
A: interest-earning money. B: basic
rule. C: school head.

6. flout ('flowt) *v.*—A: display
proudly. B: scorn. C: defeat decisively.

7. discrete (dis-'kreet) *adj.*—
A: separate and distinct. B: showing
good manners. C: whole and
undamaged.

8. ingenuous (in-'jen-yew-us)
adj.—A: showing innocence or
simplicity. B: extremely clever.
C: one-of-a-kind.

9. cachet (ka-'shay) *n.*— A: secret
stockpile. B: perfumed bag.
C: prestige.

10. allusion (uh-'lew-zhun) *n.*—
A: misleading image or perception.
B: crazy idea. C: indirect reference.

11. reticent ('reh-tuh-sent)
adj.—A: inclined to keep silent.
B: reluctant. C: backward.

12. bemused (bih-'myuzd) *adj.*—
A: entertained. B: puzzled.
C: inspired.

13. diffuse (di-'fyuz) *v.*—A: make
less dangerous. B: come together.
C: spread or pour out freely.

14. eminent ('eh-muh-nent)
adj.—A: prominent. B: about to
happen. C: inherent.

15. apprise (uh-'priyz) *v.*—
A: estimate a value. B: promote.
C: inform of or give notice.

"Verbal Misuse and Abuse" Answers

1. noisome—[B] stinky. Because of its deceptive root, *noisome* is often confused with *noisy*.

2. enervated—[A] lacking energy. From the sound of it, you'd think *enervated* means "full of energy"—nope, it's the exact opposite.

3. proscribe—[C] forbid. Careful: *Prescribe* means "to dispense a drug."

4. nonplussed—[A] baffled. The *non* is the deceiver here, leading many to equate *nonplussed* with *calm*.

5. principle—[B] basic rule. A classic gaffe. Sibling *principal* is the head of a school (think "pal") or a capital sum.

6. flout—[B] scorn. Though some sources are doing away with the distinction, *flout* doesn't mean "to flaunt," i.e., "to show off."

7. discrete—[A] separate and distinct. This is a spell-check snafu. Its homonym, *discreet*, means "prudent."

8. ingenuous—[A] showing innocence or simplicity. Not—we repeat—not *ingenious*, "showing an aptitude."

9. cachet—[C] prestige. What a difference a letter makes: Lop off the *t*, and you've got "a secret stockpile" or "a short-lived computer memory."

10. allusion—[C] indirect reference. Another infamous faux pas. *Illusion* is the one referring to a sleight of hand.

11. reticent—[A] inclined to keep silent. It's in the ballpark with *reluctant*, or "unwilling," so be reticent if you're unsure of the difference.

12. bemused—[B] puzzled. As with *noisome*, you may *want* this to mean "entertained." But as the Rolling Stones said, "You can't always get ..."

13. diffuse—[C] spread or pour out freely. You defuse a bomb or a heated situation, but a photographer might diffuse light.

14. eminent—[A] prominent. It's typically mistaken for *imminent*, or "about to happen."

15. apprise—[C] inform of or give notice. The president is apprised of a crisis; antiques are appraised (given an estimated value).

IS IT IRONIC?

Strictly speaking, irony involves a reversal. A traffic cop who has 13 unpaid traffic tickets is ironic because that is not expected. Rain on a wedding day may be dampening, and a tall man named Tallman might be coincidental—but it's properly ironic only if the rain falls on a sun festival or if Mr. Tallman is short.

FEELING YOUNG

The most sophisticated people I know—
inside they are all children.
—JIM HENSON

"

Adults are always asking children what
they want to be when they grow up because
they're looking for ideas.
—PAULA POUNDSTONE

"

The key to successful aging is to pay
as little attention to it as possible.
—JUDITH REGAN

"

If only I'd known that one day my differentness
would be an asset, then my early life
would have been much easier.
—BETTE MIDLER

"

Youth would be an ideal state if it came
a little later in life.
—HERBERT ASQUITH

"

Everybody, no matter how old you are,
is around 24, 25 in their heart.
—BRUCE WILLIS

THE PERFECT WORDS FOR
BIRTHDAY CARDS

One of the best parts of growing older? You can flirt all you like since you've become harmless.
—LIZ SMITH

"

The more you praise and celebrate your life, the more there is in life to celebrate.
—OPRAH

"

You are only young once, but you can stay immature indefinitely.
—OGDEN NASH

"

Age is an issue of mind over matter. If you don't mind, it doesn't matter.
—MARK TWAIN

"

Middle age is the awkward period when Father Time starts catching up with Mother Nature.
—HAROLD COFFIN

There is still no cure for the common birthday.

—JOHN GLENN

"

The secret of staying young is to live honestly,
eat slowly, and lie about your age.

—LUCILLE BALL

"

Birthdays are good for you.
Statistics show that the people who
have the most live the longest.

—LARRY LORENZONI

"

Those who love deeply never grow old;
they may die of old age, but they die young.

—DOROTHY CANFIELD FISHER

"

You know you're getting old
when the candles cost
more than the cake.

—BOB HOPE

This is a sign, having a broken heart. It means we have tried for something.
—ELIZABETH GILBERT

LOVE & MARRIAGE

We can't live without love, but often living with it isn't that easy either. Gaining insight from different perspectives helps us understand our own relationships and be thankful for the one we've got.

MEN ON MARRIAGE

Being a good husband is like being a stand-up comic. You need 10 years before you can even call yourself a beginner.

—JERRY SEINFELD

"

As a man in a relationship, you have a simple choice: You can be right or you can be happy.

—RALPHIE MAY

"

They say marriages are made in heaven. But so is thunder and lightning.

—CLINT EASTWOOD

"

We accept the love we think we deserve.

—STEPHEN CHBOSKY

🐦 QUOTABLE TWEETS

No one in America should ever be afraid to walk down the street holding hands with the person they love.

@BARACKOBAMA

If you marry for money, you will earn every penny.
—DR. PHIL MCGRAW

My parents just had their 50th anniversary and they're happier than ever. They have each other's back— I think that's what it's about.
—BEN STILLER

"

Behind every great man is a woman rolling her eyes.
—JIM CARREY

"

I love being married. I was single for a long time, and I just got so sick of finishing my own sentences.
—BRIAN KILEY

"

My wife tells me that if I ever decide to leave, she's coming with me.
—JON BON JOVI

"

Never marry anyone you could not sit next to during a three-day bus trip.
—ROGER EBERT

WOMEN ON MARRIAGE

Sexiness wears thin after a while, and beauty fades, but to be married to a man who makes you laugh every day, ah, now that's a real treat.

—JOANNE WOODWARD

"

Grief is the price we pay for love.

—QUEEN ELIZABETH II

"

Marriage is very difficult. It's like a 5,000-piece jigsaw puzzle, all sky.

—CATHY LADMAN

"

The opposite of love isn't hate—it's indifference. And if you hate me, that means you still care.

—MARCIA CROSS

QUOTABLE TWEETS

Don't make mountains out of molehills. If your partner says that everything is OK, believe it.

@ASKDRRUTH

It is only when you see people looking ridiculous that you realize just how much you love them.

—AGATHA CHRISTIE

"

The three words every woman really longs to hear: I'll clean up.

—MOLLY SHANNON

"

Love is blind, but marriage is a real eye-opener.

—PAULA DEEN

"

One of the few articles of clothing that a man won't try to remove from a woman is an apron.

—MARILYN VOS SAVANT

"

Why does a woman work ten years to change a man's habits and then complain that he's not the man she married?

—BARBRA STREISAND

"

For marriage to be a success, every woman and every man should have her and his own bathroom. The end.

—CATHERINE ZETA-JONES

A LITTLE HEART

Want to improve your relationships?
See love as a verb rather than as a feeling.
—STEPHEN R. COVEY

"

I know love at first sight can work.
It happened to my parents.
—GEORGE CLOONEY

"

You know how they say we only use 10 percent of our brains? I
think we only use 10 percent of our hearts.
—OWEN WILSON

"

In a nutshell, loving someone is about
giving, not receiving.
—NICHOLAS SPARKS

 QUOTABLE TWEETS

What matter is it where you find a real love
that makes this life a little easier?
@ALECBALDWIN

To wear your heart on your sleeve isn't a very good plan. You should wear it inside, where it functions best.

—MARGARET THATCHER

That's what real love amounts to—
letting a person be what he really is.

—JIM MORRISON

"

I still believe that love is all you need.
I don't know a better message than that.

—PAUL MCCARTNEY

"

If grass can grow through cement, love can
find you at every time in your life.

—CHER

"

Love is like quicksilver in the hand.
Leave the fingers open, and it stays.
Clutch it, and it darts away.

—DOROTHY PARKER

THE PERFECT WORDS FOR
WEDDING SPEECHES

The formula for a successful relationship is simple:
Treat all disasters as if they were trivialities,
but never treat a triviality as if it were a disaster.

—QUENTIN CRISP

"

Marriage should, I think, always be a little hard
and new and strange. It should be breaking your shell
and going into another world, and a bigger one.

—ANNE MORROW LINDBERGH

"

Getting married is an incredible act of hopefulness.

—ASHLEY JUDD

"

Story writers say that love is concerned only with
young people, and the excitement and glamour of
romance end at the altar. How blind they are.
The best romance is inside marriage; the finest
love stories come after the wedding, not before.

—IRVING STONE

"

Love is a game that two can play and both win.

—EVA GABOR

VALENTINE WORDS

Before sending a card this Valentine's Day, be sure you know the language of love. Here are some words perfect for would-be Romeos and Juliets. Don't know them by heart? See the next page for answers.

1. ardent ('ar-dent) *adj.*—
A: engaged. B: lyrical. C: passionate.

2. paramour ('pa-ruh-mor) *n.*—
A: chaperone. B: lover. C: token of affection.

3. buss ('buhs) *v.*—A: kiss. B: elope. C: carve initials in a tree.

4. swain ('swayn) *n.*—A: intense crush. B: male suitor. C: gondola for two.

5. connubial (kuh-'new-bee-uhl) *adj.*—A: coy. B: of marriage. C: about the heart.

6. troth ('trawth) *n.*—A: wooden or rustic altar. B: fidelity. C: Celtic wedding ring.

7. coquettish (koh-'ket-ish) *adj.*—A: flirtatious. B: alluring. C: shy.

8. macushla (muh-'koosh-luh) *n.*—A: darling. B: fainting spell. C: best man.

9. platonic (pluh-'tah-nik) *adj.*—A: of a honeymoon. B: smitten. C: without physical desire.

10. liaison (lee-'ay-zahn) *n.*—
A: secret affair. B: exchange of vows. C: pet nickname.

11. beaux ('bohz) *n.*—
A: traditional string used to join hands in marriage. B: winks of an eye. C: boyfriends.

12. requite (rih-'kwiyt) *v.*—
A: ask for someone's hand. B: give back, as affection. C: fondly remember.

13. epistolary (ih-'pis-tuh-la-ree) *adj.*—A: serenading. B: set in an arbor. C: relating to letters.

14. philter ('fil-ter) *n.*—A: love potion. B: caress. C: family keepsake or hand-me-down.

15. cupidity (kyu-'pih-duh-tee) *n.*—A: valentine shape. B: lust or desire for wealth. C: condition of instant romance, as love at first sight.

"Valentine Words" Answers

1. ardent—[C] passionate. Though he's a native New Yorker, Peter is an *ardent* Red Sox fan.

2. paramour—[B] lover. Claire was overwhelmed by the devotion and affection of her new *paramour*.

3. buss—[A] kiss. During the bus ride, Lauren and Alex sneaked off to *buss* in the backseat.

4. swain—[B] male suitor. The princess gave a weary sigh as she awaited the entreaties of her *swains*.

5. connubial—[B] of marriage. Aside from their celebrity status, Paul Newman and Joanne Woodward were famous for their *connubial* bliss.

6. troth—[B] fidelity. "It was in this gazebo, 20 years ago, dear, that we pledged our *troth*," said Arthur.

7. coquettish—[A] flirtatious. Alison caught Dean's eye with a *coquettish* smile and nod.

8. macushla—[A] darling. In *Million Dollar Baby*, boxing trainer Clint Eastwood gave his dear protégé Hilary Swank the nickname *macushla*.

9. platonic—[C] without physical desire. I hate to disappoint the paparazzi, but my current relationships are all *platonic*.

10. liaison—[A] secret affair. The young couple stole away at midnight each evening for their *liaison*.

11. beaux—[C] boyfriends. I doubt that Sharon considers young Timothy one of her best *beaux*.

12. requite—[B] give back, as affection. Her lyrics tend toward *requited* love rather than heartbreak.

13. epistolary—[C] relating to letters. The romance between Elizabeth Barrett Browning and Robert Browning is marked by an *epistolary* trail.

14. philter—[A] love potion. Hoping for attention from my crush, I went to Madam Ava for her purported *philter*.

15. cupidity—[B] lust or desire for wealth. The testimony gave clear evidence of the *cupidity* of the accused investors.

GONE A-COURTIN' ...

You may know that *horticulture* pertains to gardening. It comes from the Latin *hortus* ("garden"). Add the prefix co- ("with") to that root, and you get both *court* (a yard) and *cohort* (a companion). In royal settings of old, and still today, a flowery yard is an ideal spot for courting a sweetheart. (A quaint old synonym of *courting* is *pitching woo*. But etymologists aren't sure where *woo* came from.)

TWO OF A KIND

Whether you're from Walla Walla, Washington, or Wagga Wagga, Australia, we double-dare you to master this month's quiz— all about words with repeating sets of letters. (Don't go gaga, though.) See the next page for answers.

1. baba ('bah-bah) *n.*—A: rum-soaked cake. B: maternal relative. C: mild bruise or scrape.

2. muumuu ('moo-moo) *n.*— A: radical militant. B: lagoon in an atoll. C: long, loose dress.

3. pupu ('poo-poo) *n.*—A: tree with yellow fruit. B: sea breeze. C: Asian appetizer.

4. chichi ('shee-shee) *adj.*—A: frigid, icy. B: loose, lanky. C: showy, frilly.

5. Isis ('eye-sis) *n.*—A: fiery river of Hades. B: Egyptian nature goddess. C: rainbow personified.

6. furfur ('fer-fer) *n.*—A: about 1.25 miles. B: dandruff. C: bow-shaped pasta.

7. tsetse ('set-see or 'teet-) *n.*— A: type of fly. B: Greek hierarchy. C: opposing force of energy or gravity.

8. chop-chop (chop-'chop) *adv.*— A: sarcastically. B: intently. C: promptly.

9. nene ('nay-nay) *n.*— A: endangered state bird of Hawaii. B: forbidden behavior. C: cheap trinket.

10. tam-tam ('tam-tam) *n.*— A: pouty look. B: gong. C: skiing maneuver.

11. chin-chin ('chin-chin) *n.*— A: broom. B: type of dog. C: salutation or toast.

12. juju ('joo-joo) *n.*—A: West African music style. B: trophy. C: candy.

13. couscous ('coos-coos) *n.*— A: semolina dish. B: Moroccan beach strip. C: Congolese dance.

14. meme ('meem) *n.*—A: perfect imitation. B: recycling symbol. C: idea or trait that spreads within a culture.

15. bulbul ('bull-bull) *n.*— A: songbird. B: knobbed head on a cane. C: croak of a male frog.

"Two of a Kind" Answers

1. baba—[A] rum-soaked cake. Nothing completes a holiday feast like Becky's homemade *baba*.

2. muumuu—[C] long, loose dress. Natalie was jealous of the authentic *muumuu* her sister brought back from her honeymoon.

3. pupu—[C] Asian appetizer. Art's favorite part of the meal? The *pupu* platter of fried shrimp and egg rolls.

4. chichi—[C] showy, frilly. As we'd predicted, Lucy got just what she wanted: an over-the-top, *chichi* engagement ring.

5. Isis—[B] Egyptian nature goddess. Certainly, Bob Dylan was inspired by the mystical *Isis* when he penned his famous song.

6. furfur—[B] dandruff. "I have a great remedy for that *furfur* on your dog's coat," Tiffany offered.

7. tsetse—[A] type of fly. Sleeping sickness, a disease marked by lethargy and confusion, is transmitted by the *tsetse* fly.

8. chop-chop—[C] promptly. Yes, the soup arrived *chop-chop*, but I seriously doubt it's homemade.

9. nene—[A] endangered state bird of Hawaii. A bird lover, Marty was delighted to see the *nene* up close during his trip.

10. tam-tam—[B] gong. Lauren was fascinated by the *tam-tam* player in the orchestra.

11. chin-chin—[C] salutation or toast. Neville looked forward to saying *"chin-chin"* to his classmates at the reunion.

12. juju—[A] West African music style. Featuring a breathtaking beat, Alec's *juju* composition relies on heavy percussion.

13. couscous—[A] semolina dish. Our family's *couscous* recipe is five generations old.

14. meme—[C] idea or trait that spreads within a culture. The abuse of the word *like* is an unfortunate *meme* dating back to the '80s.

15. bulbul—[A] songbird. The *bulbul* makes frequent appearances in Persian poetry, Emily learned during her graduate studies.

OOH LA, LA

Thousands of English words, from *archery* to *zest,* have their origins in French. Think you're a word connoisseur? Take a tour through this petite list of terms, then sashay to the next page for answers.

1. raconteur (ra-kahn-'ter) *n.*— A: skillful storyteller. B: blackmailer. C: court jester.

2. faience (fay-'ans) *n.*—A: false pretenses. B: fidelity. C: glazed pottery.

3. couturier (koo-'tuhr-ee-er) *n.*— A: head chef. B: fashion designer. C: museum guide.

4. laissez-faire (leh-say-'fair) *adj.*—A: festive. B: noninterfering. C: done by women.

5. cabal (kuh-'bahl) *n.*— A: plotting group. B: young horse. C: crystal wineglass.

6. fait accompli (fayt ah-cahm-'plee) *n.*—A: done deal. B: lucky charm. C: partner in crime.

7. au courant (oh kuh-'rahn) *adj.*—A: on the contrary. B: with cherries on top. C: up-to-date.

8. interlard (ihn-ter-'lahrd) *v.*— A: encroach on. B: vary by intermixing. C: fluctuate in weight.

9. soupçon (soop-'sohn) *n.*— A: wooden ladle. B: swindle. C: small amount.

10. milieu (meel-'yeu) *n.*— A: environment. B: thousand. C: armed force.

11. aubade (oh-'bahd) *n.*— A: gold pendant. B: babysitter. C: morning song.

12. pince-nez (pahns-'nay) *n.*— A: clipped-on eyeglasses. B: rude interruption. C: narrow hallway.

13. sangfroid (sahn-'fwah) *n.*— A: intense heat wave. B: composure under strain. C: mind reading.

14. fracas ('fray-kuhs) *n.*— A: wool scarf. B: noisy quarrel. C: utter failure.

15. roué (roo-'ay) *n.*—A: thick meat sauce. B: rakish man. C: illegal gambling game.

"Ooh La, La" Answers

1. raconteur—[A] skillful storyteller. No one would call me a *raconteur*—I tend to ramble and say "um" a lot.

2. faience—[C] glazed pottery. Catherine hoped to sell the rare *faience* she'd found at the tag sale for a huge profit.

3. couturier—[B] fashion designer. *Couturiers* such as Christian Dior and Jean-Paul Gaultier have shaped fashion history.

4. laissez-faire—[B] noninterfering. In our family, Mom's the enforcer, while Dad takes more of a *laissez-faire* attitude.

5. cabal—[A] plotting group. There's a *cabal* among the dictator's aides, who are all vying for control of the country.

6. fait accompli—[A] done deal. Well, we've painted the bedroom dark purple—it's a *fait accompli*.

7. au courant—[C] up-to-date. To stay *au courant*, Rafael snaps up all the newest apps.

8. interlard—[B] vary by intermixing. I didn't understand your film—why did you *interlard* the narrative with those bizarre dream sequences?

9. soupçon—[C] small amount. Dylan detected a *soupçon* of sarcasm in his teenage son's remark.

10. milieu—[A] environment. "The briar patch," said Brer Rabbit, "is my natural *milieu*."

11. aubade—[C] morning song. Ah, the tuneful *aubade* of my alarm!

12. pince-nez—[A] clipped-on eyeglasses. I've never understood how you keep your *pince-nez* on your nose while you dance.

13. sangfroid—[B] composure under strain. We had to admire Magda's *sangfroid* as she stood up to her obnoxious boss.

14. fracas—[B] noisy quarrel. I wouldn't call it a *fracas*. It's just a difference of opinion.

15. roué—[B] rakish man. Steer clear of that guy Casanova—he's a shameless *roué*.

WATCH YOUR TONGUE

The Académie Française, which has set the country's linguistic standards for centuries, has a special distaste for English tech terms. It nixed *e-mail* and *software* in favor of *courriel* and *logiciel*. And in 2013, francophones were urged to slash *hashtag*. The French version: *mot-dièse* (*mot* for "word," *dièse* for a musical sharp symbol).

IN SHORT

In recognition of February, the shortest month (even during a leap year), we celebrate all things diminutive. Zip through this quiz in short order, then baby step to the next page for answers.

1. transient ('tran-shee-nt or -zee-ent) *adj.*—A: short-range. B: short-handed. C: short-lived.

2. vignette (vin-'yet) *n.*—A: small glass. B: short literary sketch or scene. C: thin line.

3. bagatelle (ba-geh-'tel) *n.*—A: child's rucksack. B: cell nucleus. C: something of little value.

4. scintilla (sin-'ti-luh) *n.*—A: short vowel. B: minute amount. C: minor crime.

5. myopic (miy-'oh-pik) *adj.*—A: too tiny for the naked eye. B: shortsighted. C: early.

6. irascible (i-'ra-se-bul) *adj.*—A: small-minded. B: narrow-waisted. C: marked by a short temper.

7. expeditiously (ek-speh-'di-shes-lee) *adv.*—A: promptly and efficiently. B: incompletely. C: tersely or rudely.

8. tabard ('ta-bird) *n.*—A: short-sleeved coat. B: booklet of verses. C: dwarf evergreen.

9. arietta (ar-ee-'eh-tuh) *n.*—A: tot's playpen. B: miniature figurine. C: short melody.

10. niggling ('nih-gehling) *adj.*—A: petty. B: stunted. C: short-winded.

11. aphorism ('a-feh-ri-zuhm) *n.*—A: concise saying. B: shorthand writing. C: cut-off sentence.

12. staccato (ste-'kah-toh) *adj.*—A: of cemented fragments. B: formed into droplets. C: disconnected.

13. nib ('nib) *n.*—A: crumb on a plate. B: point of a pen. C: matter of seconds.

14. exiguous (ig-'zi-gye-wes) *adj.*—A: inadequate, scanty. B: momentary. C: reduced by one tenth.

15. truncate ('trun-kayt) *v.*—A: compress by squeezing. B: speed up. C: shorten by lopping off.

"In Short" Answers

1. transient—[C] short-lived. The first-quarter lead proved *transient*, as the Ravens racked up 42 points in the second.

2. vignette—[B] short literary sketch or scene. Dickens created characters from prose *vignettes* like little photographs.

3. bagatelle—[C] something of little value. My stories aren't prized works, just personal *bagatelles*.

4. scintilla—[B] minute amount. There's not one scintilla of evidence against my client.

5. myopic—[B] shortsighted. Kim's *myopic* view of the project surely led to its collapse.

6. irascible—[C] marked by a short temper. If Jack were any more *irascible*, he'd have smoke coming out his ears.

7. expeditiously—[A] promptly and efficiently. As a pick-me-up, a triple espresso works *expeditiously*.

8. tabard—[A] short-sleeved coat. My entire Hamlet costume consists of a wooden sword and this *tabard*.

9. arietta—[C] short melody. The goldfinch trilled an *arietta*, reminding us that spring would come soon.

10. niggling—[A] petty. Mom, you're driving me bonkers with your *niggling* complaints!

11. aphorism—[A] concise saying. My father has an *aphorism* for any situation.

12. staccato—[C] disconnected. Lucy's hilarious laugh comes in sharp, *staccato* dog barks.

13. nib—[B] point of a pen. A faulty *nib*, Beth complained, ruined her first pass at her final drawing project.

14. exiguous—[A] inadequate, scanty. Ever a big eater, Art found even the jumbo burger a bit *exiguous*.

15. truncate—[C] shorten by lopping off. According to mythology, the gruesome Procrustes would *truncate* his guests if they were too long for the bed.

OPPOSITES ATTRACT

Within the month of March, we greet the proverbial lion and lamb of weather. This quiz brings you other extremes and polar opposites. So go all out (but don't overexert yourself!), then turn the page for the answers.

1. nethermost ('neth-er-mohst) *adj.*—A: coldest. B: thinnest. C: lowest.

2. extravagant (ik-'stra-vi-gent) *adj.*—A: all gone. B: irate. C: over the top.

3. acme ('ak-mee) *n.*—A: verge. B: highest point. C: overflow.

4. culminate ('kul-mih-nayt) *v.*— A: fly into space. B: hit the bottom. C: reach a climax.

5. acute (uh-'kyoot) *adj.*— A: intense, urgent. B: tiny, insignificant. C: pretty, appealing.

6. precipice ('preh-sih-pis) *n.*— A: very steep side of a cliff. B: earliest moment. C: towering spire.

7. superlative (soo-'per-leh-tiv) *adj.*—A: outstanding. B: excessive. C: final.

8. antithesis (an-'ti-theh-sis) *n.*— A: exact opposite. B: end of time. C: extremely negative reaction.

9. surfeit ('sur-fet) *n.*—A: utter wreck. B: more than needed. C: intense heat.

10. exorbitant (ig-'zor-bih-tent) *adj.*—A: on a shore's edge. B: at a mountain's summit. C: far exceeding what is fair or reasonable.

11. overweening (oh-ver-'wee-ning) *adj.*—A: arrogant. B: too fond of food. C: severely strict.

12. optimal ('ahp-tih-mul) *adj.*— A: best. B: surplus. C: out of sight.

13. radical ('ra-di-kul) *n.*— A: supreme leader. B: extremist. C: middle-of-the-roader.

14. penultimate (peh-'nul-teh-mit) *adj.*—A: next to last. B: most recent. C: cream of the crop.

15. maximal ('mak-sih-mul) *adj.*— A: greatest possible. B: conflicting. C: most important.

16. zealotry ('ze-luh-tree) *n.*— A: extreme greed. B: overdone fervor. C: excess of noise.

"Opposites Attract" Answers

1. nethermost—[C] lowest. No one dares explore the *nethermost* dungeons of this castle.

2. extravagant—[C] over the top. How can Monty afford to throw such *extravagant* parties?

3. acme—[B] highest point. Going to the top of the Empire State Building was literally the *acme* of our trip.

4. culminate—[C] reach a climax. Nearly every scene with the Stooges in a cafeteria *culminates* in a pie fight.

5. acute—[A] intense, urgent. Joey has an *acute* hankering for chocolate.

6. precipice—[A] very steep side of a cliff. As Alex peered over the *precipice*, he developed a sudden case of acrophobia.

7. superlative—[A] outstanding. Despite Willie's *superlative* effort to catch the ball, it landed in the bleachers.

8. antithesis—[A] exact opposite. Slovenly Oscar is the *antithesis* of a neatnik.

9. surfeit—[B] more than needed. We have a *surfeit* of nachos but absolutely no salsa!

10. exorbitant—[C] far exceeding what is fair or reasonable. I nearly fainted from sticker shock when I saw the *exorbitant* price.

11. overweening—[A] arrogant. I enjoy the art class, but not Professor Prigg's *overweening* attitude.

12. optimal—[A] best. Now is not the *optimal* time to pester the boss about a raise. [Note: The synonym *optimum* is best used as a noun.]

13. radical—[B] extremist. We knew Carey loved her pup, but we didn't realize what a *radical* she was until she tattooed its face on her arm.

14. penultimate—[A] next to last. My *penultimate* finish in the marathon was my best showing ever.

15. maximal—[A] greatest possible. "OK" is *maximal* praise from that old curmudgeon. [Like *optimum*, the synonym *maximum* is best used as a noun.]

16. zealotry—[B] overdone fervor. *Zealotry* gets TV attention, but it rarely brings compromise.

EARTHLY EXTREMES

At its farthest point from the sun, Earth reaches its apogee; when nearest the sun, Earth is at its perigee. In these examples, *gee* means "Earth." Meanwhile, in Greek, *apo* means "far from," and *peri* means "near to."

MIXING AND MINGLING

The rules of social engagement are always changing. But whether you interact mouse-to-mouse or face-to-face (now, *there's* a novel idea), it helps to speak the language of social harmony. Here's a primer on words concerned with schmoozing, mixing, and mingling. Answers on next page.

1. diffident *adj.*—A: argumentative. B: unmatched. C: shy.

2. comity *n.*—A: hilarious misunderstanding. B: social harmony. C: lack of respect.

3. interlocutor *n.*—A: formal escort. B: meddler. C: person in a conversation.

4. gregarious *adj.*—A: a little tipsy. B: fond of company. C: markedly rude.

5. accost *v.*— A: aggressively approach. B: offer to pay. C: decline to join.

6. propriety *n.*—A: home of a host. B: good social form. C: tendency to gossip.

7. fulsome *adj.*— A: broad-minded. B: physically attractive. C: excessively flattering.

8. confabulate *v.*—A: chat. B: get things backward. C: greet with a hug.

9. brusque *adj.*—A: clownish. B: discourteously blunt. C: full of questions.

10. decorum *n.*—A: high praise. B: dignified behavior or speech. C: showy jewelry or makeup.

11. unctuous *adj.*—A: avoiding eye contact. B: on pins and needles. C: smug.

12. urbane *adj.*—A: suave and polished. B: known by everyone. C: pertinent to the subject.

13. malapert *adj.*—A: socially awkward. B: bold and saucy. C: disappointed.

14. audacity *n.*— A: long-windedness. B: good listening skills. C: gall.

15. genteel *adj.*— A: polite. B: macho. C: timid.

HELLO
my name is
John

"Mixing and Mingling" Answers

1. diffident—[C] shy. I would hardly call Veronica *diffident*—she's the center of attention at every party she attends.

2. comity—[B] social harmony. Ducking for cover as the food fight intensified, Millie realized all *comity* at her table was lost.

3. interlocutor—[C] person in a conversation. Ever the gentleman, Professor Windham was sure to give other *interlocutors* time to speak.

4. gregarious—[B] fond of company. Dad is so *gregarious*, it's all we can do to keep him from hugging total strangers.

5. accost—[A] aggressively approach. Ariana can't even walk across the room without someone *accosting* her for an autograph.

6. propriety—[B] good social form. "Someone should tell your daughter that *propriety* dictates that she eat her spaghetti with a fork," the hostess said, groaning.

7. fulsome—[C] excessively flattering. When meeting Bev's mom, Eddie praised her with such *fulsome* remarks that she rolled her eyes.

8. confabulate—[A] chat. Luca wants to *confabulate* a bit about the new office's blueprints.

9. brusque—[B] discourteously blunt. Alice did her best to hold her

tongue after listening to the coach's *brusque* advice.

10. decorum—[B] dignified behavior or speech. In a surprising show of *decorum*, the tipsy best man gave an endearing toast.

11. unctuous—[C] smug. Ramona, don't believe a thing that *unctuous*, money-grubbing sneak tells you.

12. urbane—[A] suave and polished. Cary's *urbane* persona was obvious as soon as he stepped into the room.

13. malapert—[B] bold and saucy. After the audition, Jenny gave the director a wink in a most *malapert* manner.

14. audacity—[C] gall. Did you hear the gossip that Eli had the *audacity* to repeat?

15. genteel—[A] polite. Clare had to remind the twins to be *genteel* around their grandparents.

COCKTAIL CONVERSATION

Do you ever toss off an impressive-sounding word at a cocktail party only to wonder: Did I get that right? The terms in this month's quiz, inspired by the book *You're Saying It Wrong* by Ross and Kathryn Petras, will make you sound like the smartest person in the room—*if* your pronunciation is correct. See the next page for answers.

1. detritus (dih-'try-tuss) *n.*—A: subtracted amount. B: debris. C: falsified claim.

2. prerogative (prih-'rah-guh-tiv) *n.*—A: educated guess. B: first choice. C: special right.

3. segue ('sehg-way) *v.*—A: transition. B: completely surround. C: begin a court case.

4. hegemony (hih-'jeh-muh-nee) *n.*—A: domination. B: smooth blend. C: large family.

5. dais ('day-iss) *n.*—A: group leader. B: garden fountain. C: raised platform.

6. kefir (keh-'feer) *n.*—A: verbal skirmish. B: fermented milk. C: painting technique.

7. peremptory (puh-'remp-tuh-ree) *adj.*—A: allowing no disagreement. B: coming first. C: walking quickly.

8. quay (kee) *n.*—A: wharf. B: small island. C: dram of brandy.

9. machination (ma-kuh-'nay-shun) *n.*—A: study of robotics. B: talkativeness. C: scheme.

10. slough (sloo) *n.*—A: soft breeze. B: heavy club. C: swamp.

11. spurious ('spyuhr-ee-us) *adj.*—A: hasty. B: fake. C: livid.

12. nuptial ('nuhp-shuhl) *adj.*—A: just starting. B: relating to marriage. C: present during all seasons.

13. coxswain ('kahk-suhn) *n.*—A: innkeeper. B: secret lover. C: sailor in charge.

14. geoduck ('goo-ee-duhk) *n.*—A: earth tremor. B: wooden footstool. C: large Pacific clam.

15. plethora ('pleh-thuh-ruh) *n.*—A: person not of noble rank. B: abundance. C: spiritual journey.

"Cocktail Conversation" Answers

1. detritus—[B] debris. People on our block are still picking up *detritus* from Billy's birthday bash.

2. prerogative—[C] special right. If Dad wants to regift his dinosaur tie, that's his *prerogative*.

3. segue—[A] transition. But enough about you; let's *segue* to the topic of snakes.

4. hegemony—[A] domination. Brian has complete *hegemony* over this Monopoly board.

5. dais—[C] raised platform. The crowd threw tomatoes at the *dais* as the mayor began her press conference.

6. kefir—[B] fermented milk. Beth always eats the same breakfast: *kefir* mixed with nuts and fruit.

7. peremptory—[A] allowing no disagreement. "I am not going to bed!" the toddler yelled in a *peremptory* tone.

8. quay—[A] wharf. Passengers waiting on the *quay* prepared to board the ferry.

9. machination—[C] scheme. Despite all his *machinations*, Wile E. Coyote can't catch Road Runner.

10. slough—[C] swamp. The *slough* is home to a variety of species, including salmon, ducks, and otters.

11. spurious—[B] fake. So that UFO sighting in Central Park turned out to be *spurious*?

12. nuptial—[B] relating to marriage. I've attached a string of tin cans to the *nuptial* sedan.

13. coxswain—[C] sailor in charge. It's traditional for a winning crew to toss its *coxswain* overboard.

14. geoduck—[C] large Pacific clam. A *geoduck* can weigh over ten pounds—and live for more than 150 years!

15. plethora—[B] abundance. Joe claims a *plethora* of proof that Bigfoot exists.

DULL AS WHICH WATER?

People often say a boring thing is *as dull as dishwater*. But before the phrase was misspoken, it was actually as *dull as ditchwater*. Most dictionaries now accept either, but here are a few phrases that are just plain wrong: *butt naked* (for *buck naked*), *hare's breath* (for *hair's breadth*), and *road to hoe* (for *row to hoe*).

DATING

You've got to date a lot of Volkswagens
before you get to your Porsche.

—DEBBY ATKINSON

Being in therapy is great.
I spend an hour just talking about myself.
It's kinda like being the guy on a date.

—CAROLINE RHEA

Falling in love and having a relationship
are two different things.

—KEANU REEVES

I don't have a girlfriend. But I do know a woman
who'd be mad at me for saying that.

—MITCH HEDBERG

 QUOTABLE TWEETS

Women fall in love on the date,
and men fall in love after the date.

@PATTISTRANGER

ANNIVERSARY TOASTS

Let there be space in your togetherness
and let the winds of the heavens dance between you.

—KAHLIL GIBRAN

"

A wedding anniversary is the celebration of love,
trust, partnership, tolerance, and tenacity.
The order varies for any given year.

—PAUL SWEENEY

"

A long marriage is two people trying to dance
a duet and two solos at the same time.

—ANNE TAYLOR FLEMING

"

A good marriage is like an incredible retirement
fund. You put everything you have into it
during your productive life, and over the years
it turns from silver to gold to platinum.

—WILLARD SCOTT

Love is what you've
been through with somebody.

—JAMES THURBER

A successful marriage requires falling in love many times, always with the same person.
—MIGNON MCLAUGHLIN

Love endures only when the lovers love many things together and not merely each other.
—WALTER LIPPMANN

"
Getting married is easy. Staying married is more difficult. Staying happily married for a lifetime should rank among the fine arts.
—ROBERTA FLACK

"
One advantage of marriage is that when you fall out of love with him or he falls out of love with you, it keeps you together until you fall in again.
—JUDITH VIORST

"
You don't marry one person; you marry three: the person you think they are, the person they are, and the person they are going to become as the result of being married to you.
—RICHARD NEEDHAM

I have the worst memory ever,
so no matter who comes up to me,
they're just like, "I can't believe you
don't remember me!" I'm like,
"Oh Dad, I'm sorry!"
—ELLEN DEGENERES

FAMILY & FRIENDS

It has been said that family is everything:
all there is, all your love, all your life.
Families, and the friends that become
as close as family, shape our worldview
and inspire us to greatness.

HEARTH & HOME

The ordinary acts we practice every day
at home are of more importance to the soul
than their simplicity might suggest.

—THOMAS MOORE

"

I still close my eyes and go home. . . .
I can always draw from that.

—DOLLY PARTON

"

One's home is like a delicious piece of pie
you order in a restaurant on a country road one
cozy evening—the best piece of pie you have ever
eaten in your life—and can never find again.

—LEMONY SNICKET

"

Home is the place where, when you have
to go there, they have to take you in.

—ROBERT FROST

"

Home lies in the things you carry with you everywhere
and not the ones that tie you down.

—PICO IYER

FAMILY FIRST

Acting is just a way of making a living;
the family is life.
—DENZEL WASHINGTON

"

No matter what you've done for yourself
or for humanity, if you can't look back on having
given love and attention to your own family,
what have you really accomplished?
—LEE IACOCCA

"

I'm not going to have a better day, a more magical
moment, than the first time I heard my daughter giggle.
—SEAN PENN

"

What is a family, after all, except memories?—
haphazard and precious as the contents
of a catchall drawer in the kitchen.
—JOYCE CAROL OATES

"

A family is a unit composed not only of
children but of men, women, an occasional
animal, and the common cold.
—OGDEN NASH

I would give everything if I could only keep my family.

—JOHNNY DEPP

"

You don't choose your family. They are God's
gift to you, as you are to them.

—DESMOND TUTU

"

Happiness is having a large, caring,
close-knit family in another city.

—GEORGE BURNS

"

Call it a clan, call it a network, call it a tribe,
call it a family. Whatever you call it,
whoever you are, you need one.

—JANE HOWARD

"

A happy family is but an earlier heaven.

—SIR JOHN BOWRING

🐦 QUOTABLE TWEETS

Your #family is depending on you.
No better reason to bring
all your game all the time.

@GRANTCARDONE

CHILDREN

Having children is like living in a frat house—
nobody sleeps, everything's broken, and
there's a lot of throwing up.

—RAY ROMANO

"

I would be most content if my children grew up
to be the kind of people who think decorating consists
mostly of building enough bookshelves.

—ANNA QUINDLEN

"

Work is the least important thing
and family is the most important.

—JERRY SEINFELD

"

Ask your child what he wants for
dinner only if he's buying.

—FRAN LEBOWITZ

"

All of us have to recognize that we owe our children
more than we have been giving them.

—HILLARY CLINTON

QUOTABLE TWEETS

@ItsMyTyme09 biggest mistake in helping underserved kids is NOT RAISING the BAR high enough. Children will believe if you believe in them.

@OPRAH

The best way to keep children at home is to make the home atmosphere pleasant— and let the air out of the tires.

—DOROTHY PARKER

"

Having five children in six years is the best training in the world for Speaker of the House.

—NANCY PELOSI

"

Just be good and kind to your children. Not only are they the future of the world, they're the ones who can sign you into the home.

—DENNIS MILLER

Kids are life's only guaranteed bona fide upside surprise.

—JACK NICHOLSON

PARENTS

You can hit my father over the head with
a chair and he won't wake up, but my mother,
all you have to do to my mother is cough
somewhere in Siberia and she'll hear you.

—J. D. SALINGER

"

A new survey found that 12 percent of parents
punish their kids by banning social-networking
sites. The other 88 percent punish their kids
by joining social-networking sites.

—JIMMY FALLON

"

Imagine if you succeeded in making the world
perfect for your children what a shock the
rest of life would be for them.

—JOYCE MAYNARD

"

A rich person should leave his kids enough to
do something, but not enough to do nothing.

—WARREN BUFFETT

"

My parents treated me like I had a brain—
which, in turn, caused me to have one.

—DIANE LANE

THE PERFECT WORDS FOR

NEW-BABY CARDS

I think, at a child's birth, if a mother could ask
a fairy godmother to endow it with
the most useful gift, that gift should be curiosity.

—ELEANOR ROOSEVELT

"

If you can give your child only one gift,
let it be enthusiasm.

—BRUCE BARTON

"

Making the decision to have a child is momentous.
It is to decide forever to have your heart go
walking around outside your body.

—ELIZABETH STONE

"

Having a baby is like falling in love again,
both with your husband and your child.

—TINA BROWN

"

Babies are bits of stardust, blown from
the hand of God. Lucky the woman who knows
the pangs of birth, for she has held a star.

—LARRY BARRATTO

GOOD GENES

You can't pick your family, but you can at least talk about them. Here are a few familial, if sometimes unfamiliar, words to bring to the next reunion. For quiz answers, turn the page.

1. filial ('fill-ee-ul) *adj.*—A: related by marriage. B: of sons and daughters. C: of brothers.

2. kith ('kith) *n.*—A: friends. B: in-laws. C: homestead.

3. agnate ('ag-nate) *adj.*—A: related on the father's side. B: descended from royalty. C: of a child with unmarried parents.

4. sororal (suh-'roar-ul) *adj.*— A: grandmotherly. B: motherly. C: sisterly.

5. cognomen (cog-'no-mun) *n.*— A: clan emblem. B: name. C: last of the male line.

6. progeny ('proj-uh-nee) *n.*— A: ancestors. B: descendants. C: extended family.

7. cousin once removed *n.*—A: your cousin's cousin. B: your cousin's child. C: your cousin's ex-spouse.

8. nepotism ('nep-uh-tiz-um) *n.*—A: marriage of first cousins. B: ninth generation. C: favoritism toward a relative.

9. congenital (kun-'jen-uh-tul) *adj.*—A: acquired in utero. B: generation-skipping. C: of a multiple birth.

10. ménage (may-'nazh) *n.*— A: marriage vow. B: household. C: golden years.

11. misopedia (miss-oh-'pee-dee-uh or my-so-) *n.*—A: hatred of children. B: middle age. C: family history.

12. pedigree ('ped-uh-gree) *n.*— A: lineage. B: inheritance. C: birth announcement.

13. avuncular (uh-'vunk- yuh-lur) *adj.*—A: without cousins. B: adopted. C: like an uncle.

14. polyandry ('pah-lee-an-dree) *n.*—A: having two or more husbands. B: having two or more children. C: having male and female traits.

15. bairn ('bayrn) *n.*—A: gap in genealogical record. B: poor relation. C: child.

"Good Genes" Answers

1. filial—[B] of sons and daughters. Francis still lives with his mother, partly out of *filial* devotion, partly out of an aversion to doing laundry.

2. kith—[A] friends. With all her *kith* and kin assembled, the bride got cold feet and fled the church.

3. agnate—[A] related on the father's side. My last name has no vowels because immigration officials misheard my *agnate* grandfather.

4. sororal—[C] sisterly. After a day of looking for Polly Pocket's shoes and refereeing *sororal* squabbles, the girls' mother collapsed onto the couch.

5. cognomen—[B] name. Eugene added the *cognomen* "the Great" to his business cards and letterhead.

6. progeny—[B] descendants. With seven siblings and all their spouses and *progeny*, we have a lot of birthdays to remember.

7. cousin once removed—[B] your cousin's child. The university allows only two commencement guests for each graduate: What am I going to tell all my great-aunts and *cousins once removed*?

8. nepotism—[C] favoritism toward a relative. When the umpire—who happened to be the base runner's dad—yelled, "Safe!" the other team cried *nepotism*.

9. congenital—[A] acquired in utero. Nathaniel told the gym teacher that he has a *congenital* heart defect just so he won't have to play dodgeball.

10. ménage—[B] household. It's not a mansion, but it's just right for our little *ménage*.

11. misopedia—[A] hatred of children. W.C. Fields, who turned *misopedia* into comedic masterpieces, once said, "I love children. Yes, if properly cooked."

12. pedigree—[A] lineage. The freshman senator has a distinguished political *pedigree*, since both her father and grandfather held public office.

13. avuncular—[C] like an uncle. The pilot's *avuncular* voice was reassuring to the nervous flier.

14. polyandry—[A] having two or more husbands. *Polyandry* is rare in human societies, mostly because women object to picking up that many socks off the floor.

15. bairn—[C] child. Duncan has been playing the bagpipes since he was a wee *bairn*.

STANDING TALL

The confidence you project hugely affects how others perceive you. Test yourself on these words about proof, opinion, and even doubt. Unsure of your answers? Turn the page to be certain you are right.

1. waffle ('wah-ful) *v.*—A: flip-flop in opinion. B: press a point firmly. C: invent a wild story.

2. conjecture (con-'jek-cher) *n.*—A: group agreement. B: guess. C: optimistic outlook.

3. equivocal (ih-'kwi-veh-kel) *adj.*—A: open to interpretations. B: firmly settled. C: in the form of a question.

4. corroborate (kuh-'rah-beh-rayt) *v.*—A: support with evidence. B: steal another's ideas. C: pretend to be sure.

5. allegation (a-lih-'gay-shun) *n.*—A: proof. B: suspicion. C: claim.

6. precarious (pri-'kar-ee-us) *adj.*—A: false. B: depending on uncertain circumstances. C: having foreknowledge.

7. expound (ik-'spownd) *v.*—A: take back. B: carefully state. C: contradict.

8. intuition (in-too-'ih-shun) *n.*—A: instinctive knowledge. B: formal teaching. C: logical paradox.

9. indubitably (in-'doo-beh-teh-blee) *adv.*—A: certainly. B: doubtfully. C: deceitfully.

10. bona fide ('boh-neh fiyd) *adj.*—A: with high hopes. B: genuine. C: in contention.

11. nebulous ('neh-byeh-les) *adj.*—A: vague. B: all-knowing. C: making a breakthrough.

12. surmise (sir-'miyz) *v.*—A: sum up. B: suppose on limited evidence. C: apply logic.

13. spurious ('spyur-ce-us) *adj.*—A: sharply worded. B: false or deceitful. C: impossible to refute.

14. tentative ('ten-teh-tiv) *adj.*—A: forceful. B: all-inclusive. C: hesitant.

15. apocryphal (uh-'pah-kreh-ful) *adj.*—A: mathematical or scientific. B: not fully developed, as an idea. C: of doubtful authenticity.

"Standing Tall" Answers

1. waffle—[A] flip-flop in opinion. Quit *waffling*: Goobers or Raisinets?!

2. conjecture—[B] guess. Whether this ladder can reach that roof's gutter is anyone's *conjecture*.

3. equivocal—[A] open to interpretations. The umpire gestured, but his meaning was *equivocal*.

4. corroborate—[A] support with evidence. "I can *corroborate* Amy's excuse," her mom said. "Here's what's left of her homework after Rufus got to it."

5. allegation—[C] claim. Please don't believe the wild *allegations* that Adrienne is making about me.

6. precarious—[B] depending on uncertain circumstances. Everyone's job is *precarious* in this poor economy.

7. expound—[B] carefully state. On the first day of school, Alex's teacher *expounded* on the basics of physics to a befuddled classroom.

8. intuition—[A] instinctive knowledge. A good private eye trusts her *intuition* on a case.

9. indubitably—[A] certainly. "These footprints, Watson," said Sherlock Holmes, "*indubitably* belong to the butler!"

10. bona fide—[B] genuine. Yet again, our AA baseball team is starting the season without a *bona fide* shortstop.

11. nebulous—[A] vague. The point of practicing seemed *nebulous* to Jill until the recital started.

12. surmise—[B] suppose on limited evidence. From your white mustache, I *surmise* that you've been drinking my milk.

13. spurious—[B] false or deceitful. Tom Sawyer played hooky using a *spurious* note from the doctor.

14. tentative—[C] hesitant. An infant's first steps are always *tentative* and awkward.

15. apocryphal—[C] of doubtful authenticity. Jake gave an *apocryphal* story about having to tough it out at summer camp.

DO YOU IMPLY OR INFER?
When you're the speaker and you suggest something indirectly, you *imply* it. When you're the listener and you draw a conclusion from what someone else says, you *infer* it. Example: If you say, "Everyone needs a good diet," a friend might *infer* that you mean her. She might say, "What are you *implying*?"

DECORATING TIPS

With spring in full swing and summer sneaking up, it's time to shake off the decor doldrums and set your inner home stylist free. Before you start testing paint chips and fabric swatches, test yourself with this month's quiz, full of words you might encounter while sprucing up. Answers on next page.

1. cabriole *n.*—A: china cabinet. B: curved furniture leg. C: tea cart.

2. trug *n.*—A: shallow basket. B: triangular jug. C: padded footrest.

3. bolster *n.*—A: comforter cover. B: bed skirt. C: long pillow.

4. pilaster *n.*—A: column jutting from a wall. B: ornate molding on ceiling. C: recessed cubbyhole.

5. torchère *n.*—A: propane fireplace. B: stand for a candlestick. C: wall-mounted light.

6. grommet *n.*—A: sliding drawer. B: eyelet to protect an opening. C: anchor chain for hanging lamps.

7. pounce *v.*—A: transfer a stencil design. B: add light. C: combine fabrics.

8. patina *n.*—A: weathered look of copper or bronze. B: two-toned floors. C: high-gloss surface.

9. finial *n.*—A: ornament at the tip of a lamp or a curtain rod. B: pull string. C: metal drawer handle.

10. organdy *n.*—A: polka-dot pattern. B: insulating lining. C: transparent muslin.

11. newel *n.*—A: sunny nook. B: central post of a circular staircase. C: arched doorway between adjoining rooms.

12. bergère *n.*—A: upholstered chair with exposed wood. B: one-armed couch. C: semicircular occasional table.

13. ceruse *n.*—A: eye-catching color. B: table runner. C: pigment composed of white lead.

14. Bauhaus *adj.*—of or relating to ... A: rococo style. B: a German school of functional design. C: an eco-friendly house.

15. incise *v.*—A: prune. B: slice. C: engrave.

"Decorating Tips" Answers

1. cabriole—[B] curved furniture leg. "That *cabriole* shape mimics Rufus's hind leg!" the collector's son boasted.

2. trug—[A] shallow basket. Barbara's handmade *trugs* are ideal for carrying flowers.

3. bolster—[C] long pillow. A pair of comfy bolsters soften the ends of a daybed.

4. pilaster—[A] column jutting from a wall. Two enormous *pilasters* flanked the entrance, dwarfing the hand-carved door.

5. torchère—[B] stand for a candlestick. "Would you mind bringing the *torchère* over here?" Dean's grandmother intoned from the dark corner.

6. grommet—[B] eyelet to protect an opening. The *grommets* jangled as I yanked open the drapes and tried to duck out.

7. pounce—[A] transfer a stencil design. Diane tried to duplicate her drawing by *pouncing* it, but the effect was lost.

8. patina—[A] weathered look of copper or bronze. "How long before the roof dulls to that fantastic *patina*?" Janice asked.

9. finial—[A] ornament at the tip of a lamp or a curtain rod. Tacky *finials* cluttered the stark window treatments.

10. organdy—[C] transparent muslin. To soften your bedroom, try *organdy* curtains—they'll filter the light.

11. newel—[B] central post of a circular staircase. The handrail is sound, but the *newel* needs replacing.

12. bergère—[A] upholstered chair with exposed wood. Invented in the 1700s, the *bergère* was designed for lounging.

13. ceruse—[C] pigment composed of white lead. Applying a *ceruse* finish may help conceal the table's flaws.

14. Bauhaus—[B] of or relating to a German school of functional design. The *Bauhaus* influence was clear in her early drawings.

15. incise—[C] engrave. A carpenter may *incise* his name into his furniture.

THE MEANING OF NAMES

The meanings of some given names (Rose, Faith, Dawn) are as plain as the nose on your face. And then there are names such as Cameron, which actually comes from the Gaelic for "crooked nose." We've compiled some of the more interesting names and their derivations here. Can you use your word smarts to guess the meanings? Turn the page for answers and etymology.

1. Sophia—A: summer rainstorm. B: great wisdom. C: tremendous wealth.

2. Felix—A: faithful. B: happy. C: catlike.

3. Dolores—A: lady of sorrows. B: maiden of mirth. C: weaver of tales.

4. Natalie—A: birthday. B: first snowstorm of the year. C: princess.

5. Quincy—A: fruit tree. B: the fifth in a series. C: belonging to an ancient family.

6. Melanie—A: circular path. B: melodious. C: dark.

7. Clement—A: warrior-like. B: studious. C: mild.

8. Philip—A: as hard as a rock. B: lover of horses. C: son of Time.

9. Sylvia—A: obsessed with beautiful things. B: inhabiting the woods. C: having clean lines.

10. Benedict—A: ruled by earthly passions. B: emancipated. C: blessed.

11. Phyllis—A: butterfly. B: waterfall. C: foliage.

12. Ursula—A: little bear. B: constellation. C: giant octopus.

13. Vincent—A: winemaker. B: conqueror. C: wandering minstrel.

14. Vera—A: evening. B: true. C: raven.

15. Chandler—A: maker of candles. B: shooter of bows. C: rider of wild hogs.

"The Meaning of Names" Answers

1. Sophia—[B] great wisdom. *Sophia* is majoring in philosophy. (Greek *sophos* = wise)

2. Felix—[B] happy. Being in love has given *Felix* a new felicity in life. (Latin *felix* = happy)

3. Dolores—[A] lady of sorrows. Why does *Dolores* always sing such dolorous dirges? (Latin *dolor* = pain)

4. Natalie—[A] birthday. Each December, *Natalie* plays an angel in her church's nativity play. (Latin *natalis* = of birth)

5. Quincy—[B] the fifth in a series. *Quincy* was the only boy among the quintuplets. (Latin *quintus* = fifth)

6. Melanie—[C] dark. Of late, *Melanie* has been in a melancholy funk. (Greek *melaina* = black, dark)

7. Clement—[C] mild. *Clement's* ballgame was postponed because of inclement weather. (Latin *clementem* = mild, gentle)

8. Philip—[B] lover of horses. On Sundays you'll find *Philip* down at the hippodrome. (Greek *philos* = friend; Greek *hippos* = horse)

9. Sylvia—[B] inhabiting the woods. *Sylvia* uprooted herself and moved to Pennsylvania. (Latin *silva* = forest)

10. Benedict—[C] blessed. Pope *Benedict* issued a benevolent edict to his followers. (Latin *bene* = well; *dictio* = speaking)

11. Phyllis—[C] foliage. If you need a lesson on chlorophyll, just talk to *Phyllis*. (Greek *phyllon* = leaf)

12. Ursula—[A] little bear. *Ursula* is telling the story of Goldilocks and her three ursine hosts. (Latin *ursa* = she-bear)

13. Vincent—[B] conqueror. *Vincent* won by a convincing margin. (Latin *vincere* = to overcome)

14. Vera—[B] true. The jury doubted the veracity of *Vera's* claim. (Latin *verus* = true)

15. Chandler—[A] maker of candles. *Chandler* keeps a candelabra on his grand piano. (Latin *candela* = candle)

ARCANE NAME GAME

Cameron isn't the only name derived from an odd physical trait: Calvin means "bald" (from the Latin *calvus*). Other monikers with curious meanings: Portia ("pig," from the Latin *porcus*) and Emily ("rival," from the Latin *aemulus*). But our favorite curious source belongs to Alfred, who was apparently "given advice by elves" (Old English *ælf* = elf, *ræd* = counsel).

SPORTING

Test your gaming vocabulary with this playful quiz. There's no harm, no foul, and no penalty for flipping to the next page for the answers.

1. aficionado (uh-fish-ee-uh-'nah-doh) *n.*—A: referee. B: expert. C: buff.

2. wheelhouse ('weel-howse) *n.*—A: batter's ideal swinging range. B: overhand pitch. C: cycling stadium.

3. laugher ('laff-er) *n.*—A: close game. B: lopsided win. C: joker in a deck.

4. gambit ('gam-bit) *n.*—A: opening maneuver. B: single inning. C: intense rival.

5. arbitrate ('ahr-bi-trayt) *v.*—A: protest a call. B: serve as umpire. C: settle for a tie.

6. chaff ('chaf) *v.*—A: tease. B: discard. C: advance a pawn.

7. thimblerig ('thim-buhl-rig) *n.*—A: party platter. B: con game. C: handspring.

8. see ('see) *v.*—A: match, as a poker bet. B: leapfrog over. C: strike and open a piñata.

9. ludic ('loo-dik) *adj.*—A: following the rules. B: playful. C: easy to learn.

10. baize ('bayz) *n.*—A: pool-table fabric. B: long-range pass. C: sculling boat.

11. maffick ('maf-ik) *v.*—A: celebrate joyfully. B: enter a raffle. C: play solitaire.

12. cat's game ('kats 'gaym) *n.*—A: tie in tic-tac-toe. B: Parcheesi. C: yo-yo trick.

13. token ('toh-kin) *n.*—A: loss of a turn. B: signal to a partner. C: game piece.

14. ruff ('ruhf) *v.*—A: sail on a new tack. B: play a trump card. C: drive a ball off the fairway.

15. hat trick ('hat 'trik) *n.*—A: fancy outfield catch. B: three hockey goals by one player. C: "grand slam" of tennis.

"Sporting" Answers

1. aficionado—[C] buff. A nascent fishing *aficionado*, Jonathan insists on using spinning lures instead of worms as bait.

2. wheelhouse—[A] batter's ideal swinging range. To his chagrin, the pitcher threw into the slugger's *wheelhouse* and cost his team a run.

3. laugher—[B] lopsided win. Even though the game was a *laugher*, the victors graciously greeted the losing team.

4. gambit—[A] opening maneuver. That sneaky *gambit* might earn you a four-move checkmate, but it will cost you willing opponents.

5. arbitrate—[B] serve as umpire. When an argument broke out over the team's last cupcake, a coach stepped in to *arbitrate*.

6. chaff—[A] tease. Chloe *chaffs* Alex each time she beats him at badminton.

7. thimblerig—[B] con game. Tom thought he could outsmart the *thimblerig*, but he lost his temper and $5.

8. see—[A] match, as a poker bet. I'll *see* your pie bet with some ice cream.

9. ludic—[B] playful. Fans of the Harlem Globetrotters enjoy their *ludic* antics on the basketball court.

10. baize—[A] pool-table fabric. Eddie is such a billiards fanatic that his man cave is carpeted in *baize*.

11. maffick—[A] celebrate joyfully. The team *mafficked* its victory by rushing the field.

12. cat's game—[A] tie in tic-tac-toe. It took a hasty, careless move to break the longstanding series of *cat's games*.

13. token—[C] game piece. My family plays Parcheesi with buttons because the official *tokens* were lost long ago.

14. ruff—[B] play a trump card. I smiled at her taunts, knowing I would *ruff* on the next hand.

15. hat trick—[B] three hockey goals by one player. After Gretzky's *hat trick*, the ice was littered with fans' caps.

SUMMER FAMILY FUN

Before you splash in a pool, bask on a beach, or putter in your garden, master this list of summertime words. You won't find a lemonade stand on the next page, but you will find answers.

1. torrid ('tohr-ihd) *adj.*— A: blooming. B: scorching. C: perspiring.

2. deluge ('dehl-yooj) *n.*— A: heavy downpour. B: squirt gun. C: greenhouse.

3. verdant ('vurh-dint) *adj.*— A: sandy. B: green. C: buggy.

4. tack (tak) *v.*—A: hook a fish. B: upend a raft. C: change direction when sailing.

5. pyrotechnics (py-ruh-'tek-niks) *n.*—A: sunspots. B: fireworks. C: heat waves.

6. chigger ('chih-ger) *n.*— A: fastball. B: biting mite. C: beer garden.

7. estivate ('eh-stuh-vayt) *v.*— A: lounge outdoors. B: nurture until grown. C: spend the summer.

8. pattypan ('pa-tee-pan) *n.*— A: playground. B: heat rash. C: summer squash.

9. alfresco (al-'freh-skoh) *adv.*—A: with cheese sauce. B: outdoors. C: in a fresh state.

10. hibachi (hih-'bah-chee) *n.*— A: raincoat. B: charcoal griller. C: Asian eggplant.

11. pergola ('per-guh-luh) *n.*— A: umbrella. B: trellis. C: paid vacation.

12. glamping ('glam-ping) *n.*— A: cave exploring. B: glamorous camping. C: sunbathing.

13. plage (plahzh) *n.*— A: lawn tennis. B: lightning strike. C: beach at a resort.

14. espadrilles ('eh-spuh-drillz) *n.*—A: rope-soled shoes. B: hedge pruners. C: pair of matching beach chairs.

15. horticulture ('hohr-tih-kul-cher) *n.*—A: seaside community. B: pond wildlife. C: science of growing plants.

"Summer Family Fun" Answers

1. torrid—[B] scorching. This has been the most *torrid* August I can remember!

2. deluge—[A] heavy downpour. Tatiana threw on her black slicker and headed out into the *deluge*.

3. verdant—[B] green. Vermont is famous for its *verdant* mountain ranges.

4. tack—[C] change direction when sailing. The catamaran had to *tack* quickly to avoid the floating debris.

5. pyrotechnics—[B] fireworks. Every Fourth of July, my neighbors set off *pyrotechnics* in their yard until three a.m.

6. chigger—[B] biting mite. Miranda doused herself in bug spray before her hike to ward off *chiggers*.

7. estivate—[C] spend the summer. After hockey season ends, the Myers family *estivates* by the ocean.

8. pattypan—[C] summer squash. Has that pesky rabbit been nibbling my *pattypan* again?

9. alfresco—[B] outdoors. "Whose idea was it to dine *alfresco*?" Ira grumbled, flicking an ant off his sandwich.

10. hibachi—[B] charcoal griller. Come on over—I'm going to throw some burgers on the *hibachi* tonight.

11. pergola—[B] trellis. Legend has it that couples who kiss under this *pergola* will live happily ever after.

12. glamping—[B] glamorous camping. Hayden goes *glamping* with every amenity, then tells everyone he "roughed it."

13. plage—[C] beach at a resort. I never hit the *plage* until I'm completely slathered in sunscreen.

14. espadrilles—[A] rope-soled shoes. Melissa used to live in flip-flops every summer, but now she prefers *espadrilles*.

15. horticulture—[C] science of growing plants. The coveted *Horticulture* Award is a statuette of a green thumb.

THE IDIOMS OF SUMMER

When it comes to coining notable phrases, baseball is *in a league of its own*. If you think that claim is *off base*, we'll list the evidence *right off the bat*. Consider *in the ballpark, throw a curveball, pinch-hit*, and every shopper's favorite: *rain check*. Still think we haven't *covered our bases*? Then *step up to the plate* and name another sport that has hit more syntactical home runs.

GAME NIGHT

Puzzles and games, mind-benders and puns—they're all unleashed in this quiz. For answers and a clerihew (cleriwhat???), turn the page.

1. pangram *n.*—A: jumble of a word's letters. B: phrase using all 26 letters of the alphabet. C: person's surname used as a common noun.

2. spoonerism *n.*—A: saying "wabbit" for "rabbit." B: saying "right lane" for "light rain." C: saying "I scream" for "ice cream."

3. palindrome *n.*—A: writing that omits the letter e. B: earliest Latin acrostic puzzle. C: text that reads the same in reverse.

4. portmanteau word *n.*—A: French word playfully Anglicized. B: sailors' slang. C: word blend of two other words.

5. homophones *n.*—A: words with the same vowels. B: words with the same etymological root. C: words with the same pronunciation.

6. retronym *n.*—A: form of mirror writing. B: modified name for an old item. C: guessing game invented by bored astronauts.

7. double entendre *n.*—A: word with two of each letter. B: word identical in two different languages. C: term with an extra, often racy meaning.

8. malapropism *n.*—A: comic misuse of language. B: misspelled word. C: polite word used to replace a rude one.

9. neologism *n.*- -A: made-up or coined word. B: word that has changed its meaning over time. C: long word with a short word tucked inside.

10. cruciverbalist *n.*—A: lover of crossword puzzles. B: speaker of many different languages. C: punster.

11. paronomasia *n.*—A: tongue twister. B: pantomime skit. C: pun.

"Game Night" Answers

1. pangram—[B] phrase using all 26 letters of the alphabet. Watch *Jeopardy!*, Alex Trebek's fun TV quiz game.

2. spoonerism—[B] saying "right lane" for "light rain." I'm obsessed with lopping sweaters—er, swapping letters.

3. palindrome—[C] text that reads the same in reverse. Straw? No, too stupid a fad—I put soot on warts.

4. portmanteau word—[C] word blend of two other words. I had to chortle (chuckle + snort) while having brunch (breakfast + lunch) in the smog (smoke + fog).

5. homophones—[C] words with the same pronunciation. You've heard of my herd? The flocks eat phlox, but the ewes use yews.

6. retronym—[B] modified name for an old item. Sid wears an analog watch and plays acoustic guitar.

7. double entendre—[C] term with an extra, often racy meaning. In a nudist camp, men and women freely air their differences.

8. malapropism—[A] comic misuse of language (named after Richard Sheridan's character Mrs. Malaprop in *The Rivals*). What are you incinerating, that I'll fade into Bolivian?

9. neologism—[A] made-up or coined word. She just had a big brainstorm—she calls it a psychlone.

10. cruciverbalist—[A] lover of crossword puzzles. I shun *cruciverbalists*. They're either cross or down.

11. paronomasia—[C] pun. Regarding beetles, I always choose the lesser of two weevils.

HOT WORD

A *Clerihew* is a four-line poem that pokes fun at the famous. Invented by British writer Edmund Clerihew Bentley (1875–1956), these mini-verses have three rules: They rhyme aabb, they're about a celebrity named in the first line, and as for the meter? There are no rules! Here's an example:

Actor Harrison Ford / Was feeling extraordinarily bored. / So he grabbed his hat and picked up his bones / And starred in yet another *Indiana Jones*.

FRIENDS

A true friend is one who overlooks your failures
and tolerates your successes.
—DOUG LARSON

"

A real friend is one who walks in
when the rest of the world walks out.
—WALTER WINCHELL

"

To remember friendship is to recall
those conversations that it seemed a sin
to break off: the ones that made the sacrifice
of the following day a trivial one.
—CHRISTOPHER HITCHENS

"

You can always tell a real friend: when
you make a fool of yourself, he doesn't feel
you've done a permanent job.
—LAURENCE PETER

"

You don't have to have anything in common
with people you've known since you were five.
With old friends, you've got your
whole life in common.
—LYLE LOVETT

THE PERFECT WORDS FOR
FRIENDSHIP

The bird a nest, the spider a web, man friendship.
—WILLIAM BLAKE

"

Strangers are friends that you have yet to meet.
—ROBERTA LIEBERMAN

"

Be slow in choosing a friend, slower in changing.
—BENJAMIN FRANKLIN

"

The most called-upon prerequisite of a friend
is an accessible ear.
—MAYA ANGELOU

"

Some of the most rewarding and beautiful
moments of a friendship happen in the unforeseen
open spaces between planned activities. It is
important that you allow these spaces to exist.
—CHRISTINE LEEFELDT AND ERNEST CALLENBACH

"

A friend is someone who can see through
you and still enjoys the show.
—FARMERS' ALMANAC

Friends are those rare people who ask how
we are and then wait to hear the answer.

—ED CUNNINGHAM

"

We love those who know the worst of us
and don't turn their faces away.

—WALKER PERCY

"

No man can be called friendless when he has
God and the companionship of good books.

—ELIZABETH BARRETT BROWNING

"

I value the friend who for me finds time
on his calendar, but I cherish the friend who
for me does not consult his calendar.

—ROBERT BRAULT

"

Don't make friends who are comfortable to be with.
Make friends who will force you to lever yourself up.

—THOMAS J. WATSON SR.

We cherish our friends not for
the ability to amuse us, but for
our ability to amuse them.

—THOMAS J. WATSON SR.

There's only now.
—BILL MURRAY

LIFE IS GOOD

Hard work pays off in the moments
that are filled with beauty—
the ones that allow us to sit back,
take a deep breath, and elate in that
which we truly enjoy.

KICKING BACK

There's never enough time to do all the nothing you want.
—BILL WATTERSON

"

For fast-acting relief, try slowing down.
—LILY TOMLIN

"

Sometimes the most important thing in a whole day
is the rest we take between two deep breaths.
—ETTY HILLESUM

"

Doing nothing is very hard to do—you never
know when you're finished.
—LESLIE NIELSEN

"

Bed is like the womb, only drier
and with better TV reception.
—LINDA RICHMAN

🐦 QUOTABLE TWEETS

Life is supposed to be fun!
When you're having fun,
you feel great and you receive great things!
@BYRNERHONDA

How many inner resources one needs to tolerate
a life of leisure without fatigue.
—NATALIE CLIFFORD BARNEY

"

Time you enjoy wasting was not wasted.
—JOHN LENNON

A GOOD MEAL

There is no love sincerer than the love of food.
—GEORGE BERNARD SHAW

"

The only time to eat diet food is while
you're waiting for the steak to cook.
—JULIA CHILD

"

The trouble with eating Italian food is that
five or six days later, you're hungry again.
—GEORGE MILLER

"

Large, naked, raw carrots are acceptable
as food only to those who live
in hutches eagerly awaiting Easter.
—FRAN LEBOWITZ

A good slice of pizza can be as good
as a $200 meal in a restaurant.

—BENICIO DEL TORO

"

Life is too short to drink the house wine.

—HELEN THOMAS

"

Just try to be angry with someone
who fed you something delicious.

—CARMEN COOK

"

Stress cannot exist in the presence of a pie.

—DAVID MAMET

TRAVEL & VACATIONS

Not all those who wander are lost.

—J. R. R. TOLKIEN

"

Travel is fatal to prejudice, bigotry,
and narrow-mindedness.

—MARK TWAIN

"

I'm still ready to go to the moon, if they'll take me.

—WALTER CRONKITE

You knows what's amazing about life. Enjoying what you see.

@DENNISRODMAN

Airplane travel is nature's way of making
you look like your passport photo.
—AL GORE

"

Most of American life is driving somewhere and then
driving back wondering why the hell you went.
—JOHN UPDIKE

"

If you don't know where you're going,
any road will take you there.
—LEWIS CARROLL

"

Travel is glamorous only in retrospect.
—PAUL THEROUX

"

Camping: nature's way of promoting the motel industry.
—DAVE BARRY

HOLIDAY TIME

No matter how carefully you stored the lights last year, they will be snarled again this Christmas.

—ROBERT KIRBY

"

Christmas: It's the only religious holiday that's also a federal holiday. That way, Christians can go to their services, and everyone else can sit at home and reflect on the true meaning of the separation of church and state.

—SAMANTHA BEE

"

Christmas is a time when everybody wants his past forgotten and his present remembered.

—PHYLLIS DILLER

"

Oh, joy, Christmas Eve. By this time tomorrow, millions of Americans, knee-deep in tinsel and wrapping paper, will utter those heartfelt words: "Is this all I got?"

—KELSEY GRAMMER

I get really grinchy right up until Christmas morning.
—DAN AYKROYD

"

Oh, volunteer work! That's what I like about the holiday season. That's the true spirit of Christmas. People being helped by people other than me.
—JERRY SEINFELD

"

We're having something a little different this year for Thanksgiving. Instead of a turkey, we're having a swan. You get more stuffing.
—GEORGE CARLIN

"

Thanksgiving is the one occasion each year when gluttony becomes a patriotic duty.
—MICHAEL DRESSER

Airport screeners are now scanning holiday fruitcakes. Not even the scanners can tell what those little red things are.

—DAVID LETTERMAN

THE PERFECT WORDS FOR

HOLIDAY CARDS

May peace be your gift at Christmas
and your blessing through the year.

—UNKNOWN

"

The darkness of the whole world cannot
swallow the glowing of a candle.

—ROBERT ALTINGER

"

At Christmas play and make good cheer,
for Christmas comes but once a year.

—THOMAS TUSSER

"

Christmas gift suggestions: to your enemy,
forgiveness. To an opponent, tolerance. To a friend,
your heart. To a customer, service. To all, charity.
To every child, a good example. To yourself, respect.

—OREN ARNOLD

"

Christmas is not a time or a season but a state of
mind. To cherish peace and good will, to be plenteous
in mercy, is to have the real spirit of Christmas.

—CALVIN COOLIDGE

CAROLING, CAROLING

Carolers at the doorstep, ice scrapers working overtime, the cat swatting ornaments off the tree—the season is rife with signature sounds. In keeping with the spirit, we offer up this "aural" exam. Answers on next page.

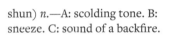

1. carillon ('ker-ch-'lahn) *n.*—A: Christmas choir. B: trombone blast. C: set of bells.

2. dulcet ('dul-set) *adj.*— A: monotonous. B: staccato. C: pleasing to the ear.

3. skirl ('skeruhl) *v.*—A: play a bagpipe. B: change musical keys. C: make a whoosh.

4. stertor ('ster-ter) *n.*—A: snoring. B: howling. C: whimpering.

5. bombinate ('bahm-beh-nayt) *v.*—A: pop like a balloon. B: bang on a gong. C: buzz.

6. euphony ('yew-feh-nee) *n.*— A: perfect pitch. B: pleasing or sweet sound. C: solo singing.

7. cacophony (ka-'kawf-oh-nee) *n.*—A: complete silence. B: audio interruption. C: harsh sound.

8. sternutation ('ster-nyu-'tay-shun) *n.*—A: scolding tone. B: sneeze. C: sound of a backfire.

9. paradiddle ('pa-reh-'di-del) *n.*— A: lilting duet. B: wrong note on a horn. C: rapid drumbeat.

10. canorous (kuh-'nor-us) *adj.*— A: honking like geese. B: echoing. C: melodious.

11. purl ('perl) *n.*—A: rippling sound. B: hum of contentment. C: heavy accent.

12. sough ('sow) *v.*—A: moan or sigh. B: squeak annoyingly. C: chug like an engine.

13. cachinnate ('ka-keh-nayt) *v.*— A: laugh loudly. B: eavesdrop. C: sizzle.

14. clarion ('klehr-ee-uhn) *adj.*— A: fast, as a song. B: repeated, as a verse. C: brilliantly clear.

15. strident ('striy-dnt) *adj.*—A: full of static. B: discordant. C: hard to discern.

"Caroling, Caroling" Answers

1. carillon—[C] set of bells. By far the highlight of the Christmas concert was the debut of the hall's restored *carillon*.

2. dulcet—[C] pleasing to the ear. Bev's tones are so *dulcet*, Jerry sat mesmerized for the entire afternoon.

3. skirl—[A] play a bagpipe. We awoke the next morning to Jimmy *skirling* away on his new gift.

4. stertor—[A] snoring. When Uncle Hal naps, the *stertor* could blow shingles off the roof.

5. bombinate—[C] buzz. The lackluster rehearsal *bombinated* in his head for the rest of the week.

6. euphony—[B] pleasing or sweet sound. There is no *euphony* like the words "Kids, time for bed!"

7. cacophony—[C] harsh sound. Nor is there any *cacophony* like the 4 a.m. pronouncement "Dad, Santa came! Santa came!"

8. sternutation—[B] sneeze. With one impressive *sternutation*, Maggie sent the startled pup ducking for cover.

9. paradiddle—[C] rapid drumbeat. "I truly appreciate Zack's devotion and practice habits, but that *paradiddle* is going to be the end of me," cried his mom.

10. canorous—[C] melodious. To Dale, the tearing of wrapping paper is the most *canorous* sound imaginable.

11. purl—[A] rippling sound. Hampered by writer's block, Alison finally found inspiration in the simple *purl* of the mountain brook.

12. sough—[A] moan or sigh. *Soughing* as loud as she could, Kate dropped off yet another plate of hors d'oeuvres for her husband's "guests."

13. cachinnate—[A] laugh loudly. I say, didn't you think Beth was overly *cachinnating* about her good fortune?

14. clarion—[C] brilliantly clear. I was enraptured by the opera thanks to the soprano's *clarion* voice.

15. strident—[B] discordant. To say Alex's new punk band is a touch *strident* is a mild understatement.

WORDS TO TRAVEL BY

Before you start cramming your suitcase for that dream getaway, make sure you've got the travel lingo down. Take a tour of these terms, then jet to the next page for answers.

1. docent ('doh-sent) *n.*—A: tour guide. B: side trip. C: frequent flier.

2. sojourn ('soh-jern) *v.*—A: travel nonstop. B: take a guided tour. C: stay temporarily.

3. cosmopolitan (kahz-meh-'pah-leh-tin) *adj.*—A: between stops. B: worldly wise. C: of space travel.

4. prix fixe ('pree feeks or fiks) *n.*—A: confirmed reservation. B: meal with a set price. C: race car.

5. couchette (koo-'shet) *n.*—A: round-trip ticket. B: French pastry. C: train's sleeping compartment.

6. funicular (fyu-'nih-kye-ler) *n.*—A: pleasure cruise. B: cable railway. C: stretch limousine.

7. jitney ('jit-nee) *n.*—A: day trip. B: duty-free shop. C: small bus.

8. valise (vuh-'lees) *n.*—A: car parker. B: small suitcase. C: country cottage.

9. sabbatical (seh-'ba-ti-kul) *n.*—A: break from work. B: lodging overseas. C: seating upgrade.

10. ramada (ruh-'mah-duh) *n.*—A: shelter with open sides. B: dude ranch. C: in-house maid service.

11. incidental (in-seh-'den-tul) *adj.*—A: waiting in a long line. B: minor. C: causing a scandal.

12. transient ('tran-shee- or zee-ent) *adj.*—A: going by rail. B: passing through. C: on foot.

13. manifest ('ma-neh-fest) *n.*—A: red-eye flight. B: reservation. C: passenger list.

14. rack rate ('rak rayt) *n.*—A: overhead-luggage charge. B: takeoff speed. C: full price for lodging.

15. peripatetic (per-uh-puh-'teh-tik) *adj.*—A: speaking many languages. B: traveling from place to place. C: crossing a border illegally.

"Words to Travel By" Answers

1. docent—[A] tour guide. I followed a *docent* through the museum, pretending to be with a school group.

2. sojourn—[C] stay temporarily. "Will you *sojourn* with us long?" asked the receptionist as I reclined on a bench.

3. cosmopolitan—[B] worldly wise. Apparently, Sara wasn't *cosmopolitan* enough for the maître d' to seat her at any of the best tables.

4. prix fixe—[B] meal with a set price. Alison knew it was a *prix fixe*, but naturally she tried to haggle with the waiter anyway.

5. couchette—[C] train's sleeping compartment. My *couchette* mates snored peacefully in their bunks.

6. funicular—[B] cable railway. The *funicular* disappeared into the mist halfway up the mountain.

7. jitney—[C] small bus. We chartered a *jitney* for our trip to the cape.

8. valise—[B] small suitcase. Eric grew suspicious after finding someone else's credentials in his *valise*.

9. sabbatical—[A] break from work. "I'm here on a six-month *sabbatical*," I tried to explain to the customs agent.

10. ramada—[A] shelter with open sides. My ideal vacation: sipping some colorful cocktail seaside under a *ramada*.

11. incidental—[B] minor. "*Incidental* items can add weight quickly, so pack wisely," my wife advised.

12. transient—[B] passing through. Thankfully, the brute was a *transient* customer, not a permanent guest.

13. manifest—[C] passenger list. I came from such a big family, we had to keep an official *manifest* for every trip.

14. rack rate—[C] full price for lodging. Savvy travelers never settle for a hotel's *rack rate*.

15. peripatetic—[B] traveling from place to place. After two *peripatetic* years in Asia, Jason settled down.

DOWNTIME, REDEFINED

These days, vacations come in myriad forms. A *staycation* is when you don't go anywhere and just enjoy free time at or near home. A *paycation* is when you moonlight as you travel. A *daycation* is a 24-hour getaway. We've also heard of a *praycation* (a religious trip) and even a *bakeation* (a foodie's holiday dedicated to sampling pastries).

EAT YOUR WORDS

Gastronomy—the art of eating—is a rich source of vocabulary in all languages (Italians have far more words for pasta than Eskimos have for snow). See how many culinary words you know, even if you can't boil water. For answers, turn the page.

1. eupeptic (yoo-'pep-tick) *adj.*— A: perfectly ripe. B: having a peppery flavor. C: promoting good digestion.

2. dim sum ('dim 'soom or 'sum) *n.*—A: dark meat of a duck. B: made with a blended soy sauce. C: small portions of a variety of foods.

3. sommelier (sum-ull-'yay) *n.*— A: wine steward. B: head chef. C: light salad dressing.

4. dredge ('drej) *v.*—A: lightly coat, as with flour. B: grind into meal. C: bind the wings and legs of a fowl.

5. Florentine ('floor-un-teen or -tine) *adj.*—A: prepared with a cream sauce. B: prepared with spinach. C: prepared with mozzarella.

6. julienne (joo-lee-'en or zhoo-) *v.*—A: season with herbs. B: steam. C: cut into thin strips.

7. roux ('roo) *n.*—A: spicy stew containing okra. B: bead-shaped grain. C: thickener for sauces.

8. coddle ('cod-dull) *v.*— A: unmold

candy. B: beat with a whisk. C: cook gently in hot water.

9. bain-marie (ban-muh-'ree) *n.*—A: cheese slicer. B: double boiler's lower pot. C: small pastry tip for icing petits fours.

10. nori ('noh-ree or 'nor-ee) *n.*— A: dipping bowls. B: seaweed wrapper for sushi. C: drink made from fermented rice.

11. macerate ('mass-uh-rate) *v.*— A: sizzle. B: soften by steeping. C: break into crumbs.

12. tandoori (tahn-'dure-ee) *adj.*—A: flavored with curries. B: sweetened with tamarind. C: roasted in a charcoal oven.

13. trencherman ('tren-chur-mun) *n.*—A: hearty eater. B: salad chef. C: waiter's assistant.

14. clabber ('clab-ur) *n.*—A: gristle. B: curdled milk. C: corn whiskey.

15. sapid ('sap-ud) *adj.*—A: flavorful. B: syrupy. C: stale.

"Eat Your Words" Answers

1. eupeptic—[C] promoting good digestion. Dad claims that watching the Super Bowl after a big meal is *eupeptic*.

2. dim sum—[C] small portions of a variety of foods. It's not worth it to take Paige out for *dim sum*—one dumpling and she's full.

3. sommelier—[A] wine steward. When Harry ordered a wine spritzer, the *sommelier* turned pale.

4. dredge—[A] lightly coat, as with flour. Rodney *dredged* everything in the kitchen but the chicken.

5. Florentine—[B] prepared with spinach. We don't use the word "spinach" in front of our five-year-old; instead we call it a *Florentine* dish.

6. julienne—[C] cut into thin strips. The puppy methodically *julienned* every pillow in the house.

7. roux—[C] thickener for sauces. If the gravy won't pour, you've used too much *roux*.

8. coddle—[C] cook gently in hot water. His joke's punch line was "Cannibals don't *coddle* their children."

9. bain-marie—[B] double boiler's lower pot. I won't make any recipe that calls for a *bain-marie*—my most exotic kitchen utensil is a pizza cutter.

10. nori—[B] seaweed wrapper for sushi. In his full-body wet

suit, Uncle Ned emerged from the water looking like a jumbo shrimp wrapped in *nori*.

11. macerate—[B] soften by steeping. For dessert, our hostess served Anjou pears *macerated* in 25-year-old Armagnac, but we would have preferred Twinkies.

12. tandoori—[C] roasted in a charcoal oven. The restaurant's unrestrained menu included both steak fajitas and *tandoori* chicken.

13. trencherman—[A] hearty eater. Our teenage son, with his *trencherman's* appetite, will eat us out of house and home.

14. clabber—[B] curdled milk. Searching the fridge shelves for a little milk for my coffee, I found only a carton full of *clabber*.

15. sapid—[A] flavorful. This soup is about as sapid as dishwater.

WALTZING THROUGH LIFE

This month we premiere an eclectic medley of musical terms—some classical, some modern, and some slangy. If you're missing a few beats, waltz over to the next page for answers.

1. clam (klam) *n.*—A: silent measure. B: wrong note. C: set of maracas.

2. legato (lih-'gah-toh) *adv.*— A: smoothly. B: quickly. C: loudly.

3. woodshed ('wood-shehd) *v.*— A: serenade. B: drum loudly. C: practice an instrument.

4. busk (busk) *v.*—A: sing baritone. B: work as an accompanist. C: play for donations.

5. ska (skah) *n.*—A: hip-hop club. B: microphone stand. C: Jamaican music.

6. nonet (noh-'net) *n.*—A: ditty for kids. B: composition for nine voices. C: unrehearsed performance.

7. pipes (piyps) *n.*—A: singing voice. B: tuba mouthpieces. C: emcees.

8. da capo (dah 'kah-poh) *adv.*— A: from the top. B: up-tempo. C: raised a half step.

9. beatboxer ('beet-bok-ser) *n.*— A: band competition. B: vocal percussionist. C: instrument case.

10. barrelhouse ('bear-el-hous) *n.*—A: bass trombone. B: rhythmic style of jazz. C: drumroll.

11. tonic ('tah-nik) *n.*—A: first tone of a scale. B: counterpoint. C: harmony.

12. noodle ('noo-duhl) *v.*— A: change key. B: croon. C: improvise casually.

13. hook (hook) *n.*—A: stolen lyric. B: saxophone line. C: catchy musical phrase.

14. skiffle ('skih-ful) *n.*—A: swing step. B: music played on rudimentary instruments. C: fast tempo.

15. earworm ('eer-wurm) *n.*— A: bassoon. B: tune that repeats in one's head. C: power chord.

"Waltzing Through Life" Answers

1. clam—[B] wrong note. Emmett's violin solo was going wonderfully—until he hit a *clam*.

2. legato—[A] smoothly. Lullabies should always be sung *legato*.

3. woodshed—[C] practice an instrument. If Lydia wants to make it to Carnegie Hall, she needs to *woodshed* a lot more often.

4. busk—[C] play for donations. I'm between gigs right now, unless you count *busking* in the park.

5. ska—[C] Jamaican music. Blake's *ska* band is holding open auditions for horn players this weekend.

6. nonet—[B] composition for nine voices. Our baseball team is also a singing group; we perform only *nonets*!

7. pipes—[A] singing voice. Brandon killed "Livin' on a Prayer" at karaoke last night—who knew he had such great *pipes*?

8. da capo—[A] from the top. Even though the score said *da capo*, the bandleader enjoyed bellowing to his musicians, "Take it from the top!"

9. beatboxer—[B] vocal percussionist. Marina is such an amazing *beatboxer* that you'd swear there was a drummer in the room.

10. barrelhouse—[B] rhythmic style of jazz. Cynthia played an old *barrelhouse* tune on the piano.

11. tonic—[A] first tone of a scale. "This concerto is in C major, so the *tonic* is C," the professor explained.

12. noodle—[C] improvise casually. I was just *noodling* around on my guitar when I wrote this riff.

13. hook—[C] catchy musical phrase. The Beatles had an undeniable knack for melodic *hooks*.

14. skiffle—[B] music played on rudimentary instruments. Our family *skiffle* band features Mom on kazoo, Dad on washboard, and Uncle John on slide whistle.

15. earworm—[B] tune that repeats in one's head. That TV jingle has become my latest *earworm*, and it's driving me crazy!

SING, SING, SING

Many vocal terms have their roots in the Latin verb *cantare* ("to sing"). *Cantatas* are pieces for singers, and *bel canto* (literally "beautiful singing" in Italian) is operatic singing. A *chanson* is a cabaret song, and its female singer is a *chanteuse*. Chants and incantations are often sung. And a long poem, whether recited or sung, may be divided into *cantos*.

THE PLAY'S THE THING

Americans spell it *theater*. The British spell it *theatre*. And the most annoying of us pronounce it "thee-ay-tuh." Find out how dramatic you are by seeing if you can identify all 15 of these theatrical expressions. Ladies and gentlemen, please take your seat. The quiz is about to begin… Answers on the next page.

1. odeum (oh-'dee-uhm) *n.*—A: song of praise. B: air of menace. C: classic theater or concert hall.

2. revue (ree-'vyu) *n.*—A: show consisting of loosely connected skits. B: critics' seating. C: final rehearsal.

3. downstage *adv.*—A: toward the audience. B: away from the audience. C: at an exit.

4. ad libitum (add 'lih-beh-tum) *adv.*—A: intently. B: spontaneously. C: slowly.

5. proscenium (pro-'see-nee-uhm) *n.*—A: introduction. B: list of characters. C: arched wall separating a stage from the auditorium.

6. histrionic (his-tree-'ah-nik) *adj.*—A: enacting past events. B: overly dramatic. C: villainous.

7. dramaturge ('dra-ma-terj) *n.*— A: plot. B: literary adviser and specialist. C: acting bug.

8. strike *v.*—A: hit one's mark onstage. B: disassemble a set. C: speak louder than a fellow actor.

9. scrim *n.*—A: swordfight. B: wig. C: gauze curtain.

10. Grand Guignol (grahn geen-'yol) *n.*—A: horror show. B: player piano. C: high comedy.

11. busk *v.*—A: entertain in public for donations. B: take tickets. C: forget lines.

12. stalls *n.*—A: prop closets. B: late-arriving viewers. C: front orchestra seating.

13. allegorical (a-le-'gor-i-kel) *adj.*—A: written in verse. B: with timely significance. C: having symbolic meaning.

14. flies *n.*—A: departures from the script. B: rapid dialog. C: overhead storage space.

15. pas de deux (pah 'de 'dur) *n.*—A: dance for two people. B: second act. C: encore.

"The Play's the Thing" Answers

1. odeum—[C] classic theater or concert hall. The opera troupe made its debut in the 1910 *odeum* downtown.

2. revue—[A] show consisting of loosely connected skits. I think the last *revue* I saw was *Side by Side by Sondheim.*

3. downstage—[A] toward the audience. Meryl forgot her lines and ambled *downstage* to ask the audience for suggestions.

4. ad libitum—[B] spontaneously. Discovering a man asleep in the front row, she delivered the rest of the scene *ad libitum.*

5. proscenium—[C] arched wall separating a stage from the auditorium. Rachel spotted the villain peeking out from atop the *proscenium.*

6. histrionic—[B] overly dramatic. "Your readings are needlessly *histrionic!*" the director bellowed at the diva.

7. dramaturge—[B] literary adviser and specialist. "When the lights blow, don't blame me. I'm just the *dramaturge.*"

8. strike—[B] disassemble a set.

The cast didn't at all mind helping to *strike* the set for *The Fantasticks.*

9. scrim—[C] gauze curtain. Reaching for her love from the balcony, Juliet got tangled in the *scrim.*

10. Grand Guignol—[A] horror show. The garish makeup, surreal staging, and *Grand Guignol* aesthetic was all wrong for *Oklahoma!*

11. busk—[A] entertain in public for donations. "Well, even Sutton Foster had to start somewhere," Kate's dad said when he heard his daughter was going to *busk* in subway stations.

12. stalls—[C] front orchestra seating. During the *Spider-Man* previews, viewers in the *stalls* were advised to take out falling-actor insurance.

13. allegorical—[C] having symbolic meaning. When the character named Eve said, "What do you know?" and bit an apple—was that *allegorical?*

14. flies—[C] overhead storage space. Audrey delighted in the snow onstage; her dad hoped she wouldn't spot the "flakes" falling from the *flies.*

15. pas de deux—[A] dance for two people. The revue featured a complicated *pas de deux* for Carla and Eli.

MUSEUM MOTS

Planning a visit to the Louvre, the Met, London's National Gallery, or another grand museum this summer? First take our quiz to make sure you have an artful vocabulary. Turn the page for answers.

1. graphic ('gra-fik) *adj.*—A: clearly pictured. B: sculpted of marble. C: roughly composed.

2. canon ('ka-nen) *n.*—A: string of images. B: standard for evaluation. C: negative review.

3. symmetry ('si-meh-tree) *n.*— A: framing and matting. B: balanced proportions. C: imitation.

4. cartography (kahr-'tah-gre-fee) *n.*—A: mapmaking. B: painted wagons. C: traveling exhibits.

5. panoramic (pan-oh-'ram-ik) *adj.*—A: of film artistry. B: shown in miniature. C: sweeping.

6. opaque (oh-'payk) *adj.*— A: deceptive. B: not transparent. C: molded in plaster.

7. juxtapose ('juks-tuh-pohz) *v.*— A: sit for a portrait. B: render precisely. C: place side by side.

8. kinetic (kih-'neh-tik) *adj.*— A: copied identically. B: showing movement. C: picturing countryside.

9. kitschy ('ki-chee) *adj.*—A: in a collage. B: tacky. C: macraméd.

10. baroque (buh-'rohk) *adj.*— A: highly ornamented. B: plain in style. C: traditional.

11. manifesto (ma-neh-'fes-toh) *n.*—A: statement of principles. B: gallery opening. C: watercolor technique.

12. avant-garde (ah-vahnt-'gard) *adj.*—A: retro. B: scandalous. C: cutting-edge.

13. aesthetics (es-'theh-tiks) *n.*— A: acid engravings. B: pleasing appearance. C: works in the outdoor air.

14. anthropomorphic (an-throh-puh-'mohr-fik) *adj.*—A: of cave art. B: made from clay. C: humanlike.

15. analogous (uh-'na-leh-ges) *adj.*—A: shapeless. B: made of wood. C: having a likeness.

"Museum Mots" Answers

1. graphic—[A] clearly pictured. The depiction of the embrace was a little too *graphic* for me.

2. canon—[B] standard for evaluation. Monet's works are certainly the *canon* by which to measure other Impressionist paintings.

3. symmetry—[B] balanced proportions. Ever the jokester, Dean asked, "When Picasso looked in the mirror, was his face all out of *symmetry* too?"

4. cartography—[A] mapmaking. No need to test my *cartography* skills when I've got a GPS in the car.

5. panoramic—[C] sweeping. Eric and Christine were overwhelmed by the photo's *panoramic* proportions.

6. opaque—[B] not transparent. Notice the *opaque* colors he chose for the backdrop.

7. juxtapose—[C] place side by side. Now that you've *juxtaposed* the photos, I agree—they're not at all alike.

8. kinetic—[B] showing movement. I thought someone was behind me, but it was a particularly *kinetic* statue.

9. kitschy—[B] tacky. Leo thinks anything that isn't Rembrandt is just *kitschy*.

10. baroque—[A] highly ornamented. Alex's *baroque*-inspired sketches were criticized for being too busy.

11. manifesto—[A] statement of principles. Art *manifestos* often come across as pretentious and superior.

12. avant-garde—[C] cutting-edge. Holly dropped out of school to join an *avant-garde* painting troupe.

13. aesthetics—[B] pleasing appearance. Ironically, Joziah's darker portraits most accurately captured the *aesthetics* of the city.

14. anthropomorphic—[C] humanlike. The artist combined everyday street items into an *anthropomorphic* figure.

15. analogous—[C] having a likeness. Right now, my brain is *analogous* to that flat, empty canvas.

SHORT AND SWEET

When people save tickets, clippings, or menus—items intended to last only briefly but often placed in scrapbooks—they are collecting *ephemera* (from the Greek *ephemeros*, "lasting a day"). Such items may not have been made by artists, but over time they acquire value for their place in history. And a cultural trend that passes away quickly is considered *ephemeral*.

SEAWORDY

In honor of Herman Melville and his masterpiece *Moby Dick,* we offer seafaring words. See answers on the next page.

1. natatorial (nay-tuh-'tor-ee-ul or nat-uh-) *adj.*—A: of swimming. B: of boating. C: of sunbathing.

2. shingle *n.*—A: gravelly beach. B: exposed sandbar. C: group of dolphins.

3. maillot (my-'oh or mah-'yo) *n.*—A: lace-up sandal. B: scuba mask. C: one-piece swimsuit.

4. jibe ('jybe) *v.*—A: dig for clams. B: turn a boat's stern. C: tread water.

5. dugong ('doo-gong) *n.*—A: sea cow. B: sea serpent. C: sea horse.

6. founder *v.*—A: sail. B: splash. C: sink.

7. thalassic (thuh-'lass-ick) *adj.*—A: of lighthouses. B: of sand. C: of seas and oceans.

8. ho-dad ('ho-dad) *n.*—A: lighted buoy. B: wannabe surfer. C: boardwalk food stand.

9. littoral ('lit-uh-rul) *adj.*—A: polluted. B: pertaining to mollusks. C: along a seashore.

10. sargasso (sar-'gas-oh) *n.*—A: tropical breeze. B: floating seaweed. C: warming current.

11. alee (uh-'lee) *adv.*—A: toward sea. B: ashore. C: away from the wind.

12. pike *n.*—A: perfect surfing wave. B: jackknife dive. C: waterskiing trick.

13. pelagic (puh-'laj-ick) *adj.*—A: of the open sea. B: threatening to storm. C: infected, as a sting.

14. mal de mer (mal duh 'mare) *n.*—A: seasickness. B: undertow. C: monster.

15. undulate ('un-juh-late or 'un-dyuh-) *v.*—A: raise a mainsail. B: move like waves. C: skinny-dip.

16. conchologist (konk-'ka-luh-jist) *n.*—A: shell expert. B: shark expert. C: erosion expert.

17. Davy Jones *n.*—A: lifeguards' CPR dummy. B: discoverer of Hawaiian Islands. C: the sea personified.

"Seawordy" Answers

1. natatorial—[A] of swimming. My *natatorial* specialty is the dog paddle.

2. shingle—[A] gravelly beach. "Ow! I should have worn my flip-flops," cried Walter, wincing as he crossed the *shingle*.

3. maillot—[C] one-piece swimsuit. The only good thing about that neon-green *maillot* is that you won't be hard to spot on a crowded beach.

4. jibe—[B] turn a boat's stern. As the storm intensified, we *jibed*, and the swinging boom knocked Stanley overboard.

5. dugong—[A] sea cow. He has the mild mien of a *dugong* but the grin of a shark.

6. founder—[C] sink. Helplessly, Joey watched as his remote-controlled boat capsized and *foundered*.

7. thalassic—[C] of seas and oceans. Though landlocked, the town, with its Nantucket-style houses and laid-back atmosphere, has a distinct *thalassic* feel.

8. ho-dad—('60s surfing slang) [B] wannabe surfer. He may have a righteous board, but that *ho-dad* couldn't surf in a bathtub.

9. littoral—[C] along a seashore. Walking slowly up and down the beach, the marine biologist collected samples of *littoral* flora.

10. sargasso—[B] floating seaweed. Columbus and his crew were nervous that their ships would become tangled in the sprawling *sargasso* of the North Atlantic.

11. alee—[C] away from the wind. "Hard *alee*!" shouted Grandpa, a former navy man, as he steered the Chevy around a corner.

12. pike—[B] jackknife dive. Uncle Hank's attempt at a forward double somersault *pike* ended up as a slap-tastic belly flop.

13. pelagic—[A] of the open sea. Petrels are *pelagic* birds that return to land only to breed.

14. mal de mer—[A] seasickness. Lloyd, green with *mal de mer*, looked up at Lucy gratefully as she mercifully handed him a packet of Dramamine.

15. undulate—[B] move like waves. Back onshore, Lloyd couldn't stomach even the sight of the beach grass *undulating* in the wind.

16. conchologist—[A] shell expert. An amateur *conchologist*, Edith was never happier than the day she found a rare paper nautilus shell.

17. Davy Jones—[C] the sea personified. Any old salt will tell you that *Davy Jones* is a fickle friend.

MUSIC

Country music has always been the best
shrink that 15 bucks can buy.

—DIERKS BENTLEY

"

Where words fail, music speaks.

—HANS CHRISTIAN ANDERSON

"

Every musical phrase has a purpose.
It's like talking. If you talk with a
particular purpose, people listen to you,
but if you just recite, it's not as meaningful.

—ITZHAK PERLMAN

"

Great music is as much about the space between
the notes as it is about the notes themselves.

—STING

"

I think my music is like anchovies—some
people like it, some people get nauseous.

—BARRY MANILOW

"

Talking about music is like talking about sex.
Can you describe it? Are you supposed to?

—BRUCE SPRINGSTEEN

QUOTABLE MOVIES

Love means never having to say you're sorry.
—*LOVE STORY*

"

Frankly, my dear, I don't give a damn.
—*GONE WITH THE WIND*

"

Nobody puts Baby in the corner.
—*DIRTY DANCING*

"

Carpe diem. Seize the day, boys.
Make your lives extraordinary.
—*DEAD POETS SOCIETY*

"

Gentlemen, you can't fight in here!
This is the War Room!
—*DR. STRANGELOVE*

Mama always said life was like
a box of chocolates. You never know
what you're gonna get.
—*FORREST GUMP*

You're gonna need a bigger boat.
—JAWS

Toto, I've got a feeling we're not in Kansas anymore.
—THE WIZARD OF OZ

"

I love the smell of napalm in the morning.
—APOCALYPSE NOW

"

We must all face the choice between
what is right and what is easy.
—HARRY POTTER AND THE GOBLET OF FIRE

"

It doesn't take much to see that the problems
of three little people don't amount to a hill
of beans in this crazy world.
—CASABLANCA

"

I fart in your general direction. Your mother was
a hamster and your father smelt of elderberries.
—MONTY PYTHON AND THE HOLY GRAIL

"

Leave the gun, take the cannoli.
—THE GODFATHER

I like to crack the jokes
now and again, but it's only because
I struggle with math.
—TINA FEY

A LAUGH A MINUTE

Keeping a sense of humor about life,
the universe, and everything is essential to
keeping sane. Laughter is immediate relief
for whatever ails you, and we're lucky that
there are so many notable people practicing
the therapeutic art of comedy.

LAUGHTER, THE BEST MEDICINE

If there's one thing I know, it's that
God does love a good joke.
—HUGH ELLIOTT

"

Laughter brings the swelling down
on our national psyche.
—STEPHEN COLBERT

"

I am thankful for laughter, except when
milk comes out my nose.
—WOODY ALLEN

"

Nothing to me feels as good as
laughing incredibly hard.
—STEVE CARELL

"

I wake up laughing every day. I get a kick out of life.
—BRUCE WILLIS

"

Laughter is the shortest distance between two people.
—VICTOR BORGE

Good taste is the enemy of comedy.

—MEL BROOKS

Whoever established the high road, and how
high it should be, should be fired.

—SANDRA BULLOCK

"

Tell me what you laugh at, and I'll tell you who you are.

—MARCEL PAGNOL

"

Laughter is an instant vacation.

—MILTON BERLE

"

You can't deny laughter. When it comes, it plops down
in your favorite chair and stays as long as it wants.

—STEPHEN KING

"

Comedy is like catching lightning in a bottle.

—GOLDIE HAWN

"

I'm not funny. What I am is brave.

—LUCILLE BALL

"

The only way you can know where
the line is, is if you cross it.

—DAVE CHAPPELLE

LIFE LESSONS

A synonym is a word you use when you can't spell the first word you thought of.
—BURT BACHARACH

"

It's only when the tide goes out that you learn who's been swimming naked.
—WARREN BUFFETT

"

The difference between fiction and reality? Fiction has to make sense.
—TOM CLANCY

"

When the winds of change blow, some people build walls, and others build windmills.
—CHINESE PROVERB

"

You should take your job seriously but not yourself. That is the best combination.
—DAME JUDI DENCH

"

Not being funny doesn't make you a bad person. Not having a sense of humor does.
—DAVID RAKOFF

There's no one way to dance.
And that's kind of my philosophy about everything.
—ELLEN DEGENERES

"

The trouble with having an open mind, of course,
is that people will insist on coming along and
trying to put things in it.
—TERRY PRATCHETT

"

Men don't care what's on TV.
They only care what else is on TV.
—JERRY SEINFELD

"

If there's a single lesson that life teaches us,
it's that wishing doesn't make it so.
—LEV GROSSMAN

"

You have to remember one thing about
the will of the people: It wasn't that long ago
that we were swept away by the macarena.
—JON STEWART

Without geography, you're nowhere.
—JIMMY BUFFETT

TECHNOLOGY

Because Google is so popular, it's conceited.
Have you tried misspelling something lately? See the
tone that it takes? "Um, did you mean . . . ?"

—ARJ BARKER

"

When I first heard about the campaign to get me
to host *Saturday Night Live*, I didn't know what
Facebook was. And now that I do know what it is,
I have to say, it sounds like a huge waste of time!

—BETTY WHITE

"

So I'm reading a book on my new iPad, but can't the
iPad read it for me? Do I have to do everything?

—MATTHEW PERRY

If it keeps up, man will
atrophy all his limbs
but the push-button finger.

—FRANK LLOYD WRIGHT

Personally, I'm waiting
for caller IQ.
—SANDRA BERNHARD

E-mails are letters, after all,
more lasting than phone calls,
even if many of them r 2 cursory 4 u.
—ANNA QUINDLEN

"

To err is human, but to really foul things up
you need a computer.
—PAUL EHRLICH

"

Computers make it easier to do a lot of things,
but most of the things they make easier to do
don't need to be done.
—ANDY ROONEY

"

I don't believe in e-mail. I'm an old-fashioned girl.
I prefer calling and hanging up.
—SARAH JESSICA PARKER

THE PERFECT WORDS TO

OPEN WITH A LAUGH

The human brain starts working the
moment you are born and never stops until
you stand up to speak in public.
—GEORGE JESSEL

"

A dead-end street is a good place to turn around.
—NAOMI JUDD

"

I've had a perfectly wonderful evening,
but this wasn't it.
—GROUCHO MARX

"

The problem is never how to get new,
innovative thoughts into your mind,
but how to get old ones out.
—DEE HOCK

"

It doesn't work to leap a twenty-foot
chasm in two ten-foot jumps.
—PROVERB

"

Great ideas often receive violent
opposition from mediocre minds.
—ALBERT EINSTEIN

YIDDISH FUN

Words should be weighed, not counted, goes the Yiddish proverb. Of the thousands of words English has borrowed from other languages, Yiddish loanwords are perhaps the weightiest. How many other nouns pack the precision, sarcasm, humor, and onomatopoeia into seven letters that schlump (sloppy dresser) does? For quiz answers, turn the page.

1. kvetch ('kvech) *v.*—A: cook. B: complain. C: boast.

2. zaftig ('zahf-tig) *adj.*—A: pleasantly plump. B: giddy. C: curious.

3. chutzpah ('hoot-spuh) *n.*—A: sudden attack. B: filled crepe. C: gall.

4. yenta ('yen-ta) *n.*— A: busybody. B: matchmaker. C: rabbi's wife.

5. plotz ('plots) *v.*—A: measure. B: figure out. C: collapse.

6. meshuga (muh-'shoog-uh) *adj.*— A: worthless. B: too sweet. C: daffy.

7. nebbish ('neb-ish) *n.*—A: elegantly dressed man. B: milquetoast. C: smart aleck.

8. tchotchke ('chach-kuh) *n.*— A: folk dance. B: bad memory. C: knickknack.

9. schnorrer ('shnor-ur) *n.*—A: loud sleeper. B: moocher. C: ladies' man.

10. oy vey ('oy 'vay) *interj.*— A: Happy birthday! B: Hip hip hooray! C: Oh, woe!

11. kibitz ('kib-its or kuh-'bits) *v.*—A: clean obsessively. B: tell jokes. C: offer opinions.

12. mensch ('mench) *n.*— A: coward. B: honorable person. C: ne'er-do-well.

13. schlep ('shlep) *v.*—A: haul. B: insult. C: weep.

14. nudnik ('nood-nik) *n.*—A: first-year student. B: bumpkin. C: bore.

15. bubkes ('bup-cuss) *n.*—A: stroke of luck. B: nothing. C: term of endearment.

16. shamus ('shah-mus or 'shay-) *n.*—A: detective. B: hoax. C: free-for-all.

17. mazel tov ('mah-zul 'tov) *interj.*—A: Sorry—my bad! B: Welcome home! C: Best wishes!

"Yiddish Fun" Answers

1. kvetch—[B] complain. If Bernice *kvetched* about her friends less, she might have more of them.

2. zaftig—[A] pleasantly plump. The *zaftig* beauty was the first plus-size contestant to win *America's Next Top Model*.

3. chutzpah—[C] gall. After jumping the light, the other driver had the *chutzpah* to blame me for the accident.

4. yenta—[A] busybody. The office romance provided irresistible fodder for the watercooler *yentas*.

5. plotz—[C] collapse. When my mom sees my report card, she'll *plotz*.

6. meshuga—[C] daffy. My *meshuga* neighbor has dressed his garden gnomes in flak jackets.

7. nebbish—[B] milquetoast. A *nebbish* in an ill-fitting suit, the accountant nervously said "excuse me" to the coworker blocking the fax machine.

8. tchotchke—[C] knickknack. Among the yard sale *tchotchkes*, there it was: Punchers the Lobster, one of the original Beanie Babies.

9. schnorrer—[B] moocher. That *schnorrer* Artie always forgets his wallet when we eat out.

10. oy vey—[C] Oh, woe! Dad got out of the car, looked at the flat tire, and said, "*Oy vey!*"

11. kibitz—[C] offer opinions. Jane does more *kibitzing* than helping.

12. mensch—[B] honorable person. The mayor is a *mensch*—respected even by those who disagree with him.

13. schlep—[A] haul. Lois *schlepped* the newspapers to the recycling center, realizing much later that she'd tossed her husband's prize baseball card collection.

14. nudnik—[C] bore. Don't look now, but here comes that *nudnik* from the IT department.

15. bubkes—[B] nothing. They went to Vegas with a bundle and came back with *bubkes*.

16. shamus—[A] detective. You don't have to be a *shamus* to figure out that the e-mail is a scam.

17. mazel tov—[C] Best wishes! You got the job? *Mazel tov!*

FUNNIEST ENGLISH WORDS

At long last, a quiz dedicated to plain ol' fun! Inspired by *The 100 Funniest Words in English*, by Robert Beard, these picks are all a mouthful, and some even sport serious definitions (others... well, not so much). Enjoy weaving them into your dinner-table conversation tonight. Answers on next page.

1. flummox ('fluh-muks) *v.*—
A: laugh out loud. B: confuse.
C: ridicule.

2. crudivore ('crew-dih-vor) *n.*—
A: foulmouthed person. B: garbage
can. C: eater of raw food.

3. hoosegow ('hoos-gow) *n.*—
A: jail. B: scaredy-cat. C: strong
liquor, usually moonshine.

4. mollycoddle ('mah-lee-kah-dl)
v.—A: treat with an absurd degree of
attention. B: mix unwisely. C: moo
or imitate a cow.

5. donnybrook ('dah-nee-bruk)
n.—A: rapid stream. B: wild brawl.
C: stroke of luck.

6. cantankerous (kan-'tan-keh-res)
adj.—A: very sore. B: hard to deal
with. C: obnoxiously loud.

7. codswallop ('kahdz-wah-lep)
n.—A: sound produced by a hiccup.
B: rare rainbow fish. C: nonsense.

8. doozy ('doo-zee) *n.*—
A: extraordinary one of its kind.

B: incomprehensible song. C: double
feature.

9. discombobulate (dis-kehm-'bah-
byoo-layt) *v.*—A: take apart. B: fail.
C: upset or frustrate.

10. hootenanny ('hoo-teh-na-nee)
n.—A: group of owls. B: folksinging
event. C: child's caregiver.

11. yahoo ('yah-hoo) *n.*—
A: overzealous fan. B: pratfall.
C: dumb person.

12. kerfuffle (ker-'fuh-fuhl) *n.*—
A: failure to ignite. B: down pillow
or blanket. C: disturbance.

13. absquatulate (abz-'kwah-chew-
layt) *v.*—A: abscond or flee. B: stay
low to the ground. C: utterly flatten.

14. skullduggery (skul-'duh-geh-
ree) *n.*—A: Shakespearean prank. B:
underhanded behavior.
C: graveyard.

15. flibbertigibbet (flih-ber-tee-'jih-
bet) *n.*—A: silly and flighty person.
B: snap of the fingers. C: hex or curse.

"Funniest English Words" Answers

1. flummox—[B] confuse. Sarah is easily *flummoxed* by any changes to the schedule.

2. crudivore—[C] eater of raw food. To help boost my health, I'm declaring myself a *crudivore*.

3. hoosegow—[A] jail. After protesting a touch too loudly in court, Tara found herself in the *hoosegow*.

4. mollycoddle—[A] treat with an absurd degree of attention. "Lillie's my only grandchild—I'll *mollycoddle* her all I want!"

5. donnybrook—[B] wild brawl. It took four umps to quell the *donnybrook* at home plate.

6. cantankerous—[B] hard to deal with. The comic was greeted by a *cantankerous* crowd at his debut.

7. codswallop—[C] nonsense. "Oh, *codswallop*! I never went near that bowl of candy," Dad barked.

8. doozy—[A] extraordinary one of its kind. That was a *doozy* of a

storm—luckily, we dodged the two downed trees.

9. discombobulate—[C] upset or frustrate. The goal of the simulator: *discombobulate* even the sharpest of pilots.

10. hootenanny—[B] folksinging event. After the concert, let's head up the hill for the informal *hootenanny*.

11. yahoo—[C] dumb person. Please try not to embarrass me at Sally's party, you big *yahoo*.

12. kerfuffle—[C] disturbance. I was referring to that minor *kerfuffle* called World War II.

13. absquatulate—[A] abscond or flee. Upon opening the door, Clare watched the new puppy *absquatulate* with her sneaker.

14. skullduggery—[B] underhanded behavior. The chairman was infamous for resorting to *skullduggery* during contract negotiations.

15. flibbertigibbet—[A] silly and flighty person. Do I have to spend the entire ride with that *flibbertigibbet* next to me?!

PIRATES IN THE HOUSE

Robert Beard's list of funny words also includes *filibuster*, which you probably know as a long political speech. But did you know it's also related to pirates? The Spanish *filibustero* means "freebooter," a pirate or plunderer. So you might say a *filibuster* in Congress is a way of stealing time—legislative piracy!

ABRACADABRA

A wave of our wand and presto! We conjure
a page of magical words and phrases. Step right up
and test your vocabulary—then transport yourself
to the next page, where we reveal the answers.

1. levitate ('le-vih-tayt) *v.*—A: defy
gravity. B: weave spells.
C: disappear.

2. clairvoyant (klayr-'voy-ent)
adj.—A: in a trance. B: ghostly.
C: seeing beyond ordinary
perception.

3. planchette (plan-'shet)
n.—A: sorcerer's cloak. B: Ouija
board pointer. C: mischievous fairy.

4. mojo ('moh-joh)
n.—A: book of secrets. B: magical
spell. C: mantra.

5. telekinetic (te-leh-kih-'neh-tik)
adj.—A: predicting the future.
B: calling on ghosts. C: using mind
over matter.

6. voilà (vwah-'lah)
interj.—A: "Begone!" B: "There it
is!" C: "Open!"

7. whammy ('wa-mee)
n.—A: trapdoor. B: illusion. C: hex
or curse.

8. soothsaying ('sooth-say-ing)
n.—A: prophecy. B: recitation of
chants. C: revelation of a trick.

9. mesmerized ('mez-meh-
riyzd) *adj.*—A: sawed in half. B:
hypnotized. C: turned to pixie dust.

10. augur ('ah-ger)
v.—A: serve as an omen. B: bend a
spoon without touching it. C: chant
in a monotone.

11. shaman ('shah-men)
n.—A: fake psychic. B: healer using
magic. C: genie in a bottle.

12. occult (uh-'khult)
adj.—A: sinister. B: miraculous.
C: secret.

13. invoke (in-'vohk)
v.—A: transform. B: use
ventriloquism. C: summon up, as
spirits.

14. sibyl ('si-buhl)
n.—A: séance. B: fortune-teller.
C: black cat.

15. pentagram ('pen-teh-gram)
n.—A: elixir. B: five-pointed star.
C: enchanted staff.

"Abracadabra" Answers

1. levitate—[A] defy gravity. Before dunking the basketball, Michael *levitates* long enough to polish the backboard and rim.

2. clairvoyant—[C] seeing beyond ordinary perception. As a bookie, I find being *clairvoyant* really helps me call the races.

3. planchette—[B] Ouija board pointer. My *planchette* just spelled out "You're too gullible."

4. mojo—[B] magical spell. I've got my *mojo* working, but I still can't charm Angelina.

5. telekinetic—[C] using mind over matter. Chloe employs her *telekinetic* powers to make the trash empty itself.

6. voilà—[B] "There it is!" As he threw back the curtain, Houdini cried, "*Voilà!*"

7. whammy—[C] hex or curse. After the gypsy placed a *whammy* on Tex, he fell into the duck pond three times.

8. soothsaying—[A] prophecy. If Joe is so good at *soothsaying*, why does he always lose in Vegas?

9. mesmerized—[B] hypnotized. Since meeting Jenny, Paul has been stumbling around as though *mesmerized*.

10. augur—[A] serve as an omen. A flat tire on the first day surely *augurs* ill for our vacation.

11. shaman—[B] healer using magic. The local *shaman* recited a few incantations to heal my broken nose.

12. occult—[C] secret. At midnight, I was poring over an *occult* black-magic text.

13. invoke—[C] summon up, as spirits. While studying ancient Rome, I tried to *invoke* the ghost of Caesar to appear before me.

14. sibyl—[B] fortune-teller. My apprehension grew as the *sibyl* looked into her crystal ball and winced.

15. pentagram—[B] five-pointed star. David said his spells don't work unless he traces a *pentagram* with his wand.

DIVINING DICTIONARY

When predicting the future, the suffix we use is -*mancy*, which means "divination." *Pyromancy* involves reading the future in flames, *hydromancy* in water, and *chiromancy* in the lines on the palm of a hand. Another far-out example: *favomancy*, meaning "telling the future by reading beans scattered on the ground." Related to mantra and mania, the root -*mancy* is derived from mind.

MASH-UPS

From brunch (breakfast + lunch) to Wi-Fi (wireless + fidelity), today's English language is full of hybrid words. Other examples include smog, sitcom, and Muppet, as well as those below. Enjoy the edutainment— or turn to the next page for the answers.

1. motorcade ('moh-ter-kaid) *n.*—A: breakdown. B: automatic response. C: procession of vehicles.

2. radome ('ray-dohm) *n.*—A: salad vegetable. B: antenna housing. C: all-night party.

3. digerati (di-juh-'rah-tee) *n.*— A: archaeologist. B: computer whizzes. C: screen pixels.

4. slurve ('slurv) *n.*—A: ice-cream drink. B: automobile stunt. C: baseball pitch.

5. telegenic ('te-li-je-nik) *adj.*— A: suitable manner and appearance for TV. B: having ESP. C: born on foreign soil.

6. meld ('meld) *v.*—A: liquefy. B: combine. C: harden with age.

7. bodacious (boh-'dey-shus) *adj.*—A: remarkable. B: interfering. C: part human, part machine.

8. chillax (chi-'laks) *v.*—A: ice fish.

B: calm down. C: rudely insult.

9. agitprop ('ah-jit-prop) *n.*—A: political hype. B: building support. C: crowd control.

10. bromance ('bro-mans) *n.*—A: fraternity dwelling. B: gaseous element. C: close male friendship.

11. liger ('liy-ger) *n.*—A: liquid measure. B: midnight snack. C: big cat.

12. frenemy ('fre-nuh-mee) *n.*—A: false friend. B: opposition army. C: frantic movement.

13. Frankenfood ('fran-ken-food) *n.*—A: dangerous eats. B: genetically engineered food. C: fusion cuisine.

14. mockumentary (mok-yoo-'men-tah-ree) *n.*—A: simulated-trial manual. B: placebo. C: satirical film style.

15. sysop ('siys-op) *n.*—A: online administrator. B: photo shoot. C: music overdubbing.

"Mash-Ups" Answers

1. motorcade—[C] procession of vehicles (motor + cavalcade). How many insipid celebutantes are riding in the *motorcade*?

2. radome—[B] antenna housing (radar + dome). The plucky parasailer passed over the *radome* undetected.

3. digerati—[B] computer whizzes (digital + literati). Today's mathletes will become tomorrow's *digerati*.

4. slurve—[C] baseball pitch (slider + curve). A batter can only guesstimate where A.J.'s *slurve* will go.

5. telegenic—[A] suitable manner and appearance for TV (television + photogenic). Only the most *telegenic* dancers appear on the show *So You Think You Can Jazzercise*.

6. meld—[B] combine (melt + weld). Inventors *melded* two devices to create the camcorder.

7. bodacious—[A] remarkable (bold + audacious). Wasn't it *bodacious* of Bonnie to become a paratrooper?

8. chillax—[B] calm down (chill + relax). A puzzle addict, Daniel refused to *chillax* until he solved the cryptex.

9. agitprop—[A] political hype (agitation + propaganda). No one was persuaded by the *agitprop* promulgated in the newscast.

10. bromance—[C] close male friendship (brother + romance). Ben and Andy's *bromance* grew out of their mutual love of automobilia.

11. liger—[C] big cat (lion + tiger). I can't go to the Cineplex—I have to feed my *liger*.

12. frenemy—[A] false friend (friend + enemy). A true *frenemy*, Lisa poked fun at my bob before asking her hairstylist for one too.

13. Frankenfood—[B] genetically engineered food (Frankenstein + food). The food purists plotted ecotage against the *Frankenfood* conglomerate.

14. mockumentary—[C] satirical film style (mock + documentary). Kathy urged her Labradoodle-loving sister to watch *Best in Show*, a *mockumentary* about five dog owners.

15. sysop—[A] online administrator (system + operator). A savvy *sysop* knows how to detect malware.

THE I'S HAVE IT

What do whiz kids, fish sticks, miniskirts, and film critics have in common? Their only vowel is the letter i. So grab your skim milk, put on your string bikini, and hit this list. Then try hitchhiking to the next page for answers.

1. grissini (grih-'see-nee) *n.*—
A: Italian breadsticks. B: carved inscriptions. C: figure skating jump.

2. dirndl ('dern-duhl) *n.*—
A: needle for darning. B: full skirt. C: spinning top.

3. limpid ('lihm-pihd) *adj.*—
A: hobbling. B: perfectly clear. C: like a mollusk.

4. schism ('skih-zuhm) *n.*—
A: separation. B: pithy quotation. C: deep hole.

5. kimchi ('kihm-chee) *n.*—
A: logic puzzle. B: throw rug. C: pickled dish.

6. skinflint ('skihn-flihnt) *n.*—
A: scam artist. B: penny-pincher. C: fire starter.

7. insipid (ihn-'sih-pihd) *adj.*—
A: bland. B: just getting started. C: undrinkable.

8. fizgig ('fihz-gihg) *n.*—A: plan that fails. B: large swarm of bees. C: hissing firework.

9. jib ('jihb) *n.*—A: sharpened pencil point. B: bird's beak. C: triangular sail.

10. philippic (fih-'lih-pihk) *n.*—
A: international treaty. B: charitable gift. C: tirade.

11. viscid ('vih-sid) *adj.*—
A: sticky. B: transparent. C: wickedly cruel.

12. krill ('kril) *n.*—A: tiny crustaceans. B: peacock tail feathers. C: knitting pattern.

13. pippin ('pih-pihn) *n.*—A: apple. B: migrating songbird. C: thumbtack.

14. pidgin ('pih-juhn) *n.*—
A: trapshooter's target. B: toe turned inward. C: simplified language.

15. niblick ('nih-blihk) *n.*—
A: comic routine. B: iron golf club. C: pocket flask.

"The I's Have It" Answers

1. grissini—[A] Italian breadsticks. Daryl wished the child at the next table would stop playing drums with the *grissini*.

2. dirndl—[B] full skirt. For her role in the musical, Christina is donning a *dirndl* and learning to yodel.

3. limpid—[B] perfectly clear. The water in the bay was warm and *limpid*—ideal for an afternoon of snorkeling.

4. schism—[A] separation. There is quite a *schism* between your idea of good coffee and mine.

5. kimchi—[C] pickled dish. Annie used to hate Korean food, but now *kimchi* is her favorite snack.

6. skinflint—[B] penny-pincher. Our *skinflint* of an uncle never tips a dime.

7. insipid—[A] bland. No *insipid* love ballads for this band; we're here to rock!

8. fizgig—[C] hissing firework. The wedding reception ended with a celebratory *fizgig* display.

9. jib—[C] triangular sail. Harry is an amateur when it comes to sailing—he doesn't know the *jib* from the mainsail.

10. philippic—[C] tirade. We accidentally goaded Joaquin into one of his wild *philippics* about his ex-wife.

11. viscid—[A] sticky. The massive spider in my greenhouse has caught many a hapless fly in its *viscid* snare.

12. krill—[A] tiny crustaceans. One blue whale can consume up to four tons of *krill* each day.

13. pippin—[A] apple. "Ten bucks says I can knock that *pippin* right off your head!" said William Tell.

14. pidgin—[C] simplified language. Sean isn't afraid to travel to places where he doesn't speak the native tongue—he relies on *pidgin* to communicate.

15. niblick—[B] iron golf club. Emma cursed her *niblick* as her ball splashed down in the pond near the ninth hole.

WHY WIKI?

Ever wonder how the reference site Wikipedia got its name? In 1995, programmer Ward Cunningham called a user-editable website he'd created WikiWikiWeb, after the Wiki-Wiki shuttle buses he'd seen at the Honolulu airport. (*Wikiwiki* means "quickly" in Hawaiian.) That was the very first wiki—a site that allows contributions or corrections by its users.

BATTER UP

For rookies to old-timers, benchwarmers to all-stars, our national pastime is a rich field of vocabulary. Take a hefty swing at this quiz in honor of baseball. For answers, turn the page.

1. bandbox *n.*—A: warm-up area for pitchers. B: bleacher section. C: small stadium.

2. cleanup *adj.*—A: caught on the fly. B: fourth among batters. C: scoring zero runs.

3. pickle *n.*—A: hard-to-hold bat. B: bad umpire. C: play in which a runner is caught between bases.

4. rhubarb *n.*—A: heated argument. B: razzing from fans. C: thick infield grass.

5. shag *v.*—A: steal home. B: bobble a fly ball. C: practice catching in the outfield.

6. moxie *n.*—A: team mascot. B: extra spin on a pitch. C: skill and daring.

7. Texas leaguer *n.*—A: rookie player. B: double play. C: bloop hit.

8. Baltimore chop *n.*—A: high-bouncing ground ball. B: weak swing. C: ballpark hot dog.

9. fireman *n.*—A: relief pitcher. B: groundskeeper. C: third-base coach.

10. rubber game *n.*—A: blowout. B: deciding game of a series. C: poorly played game.

11. gun down *v.*—A: throw three straight strikes. B: throw out a runner. C: throw at a batter.

12. chin music *n.*—A: dispute with an umpire. B: high inside pitch. C: hometown cheers.

13. gopher ball *n.*—A: foul fly into the stands. B: hard-hit ground ball. C: easy pitch to slug.

14. bang-bang *adj.*—A: close, as a play at a base. B: ricocheting. C: requiring both hands.

15. fungo *n.*—A: exhibition game. B: catcher's mask. C: fly ball for practice.

16. blow smoke *v.*—A: taunt. B: throw fast. C: relax on an off day.

"Batter Up" Answers

1. bandbox—[C] small stadium. No wonder Joe Bailey hit 50 homers last year—look at the dinky *bandbox* he calls a home park.

2. cleanup—[B] fourth among batters. Hinson, Rodriguez, and Pearson led off with walks, setting the stage for the Whammer, the league's top *cleanup* hitter.

3. pickle—[C] play in which a runner is caught between bases. Smalls escaped the *pickle* by taking a ball to the head.

4. rhubarb—[A] heated argument. Terry Durham and Jimmy Schnell went jaw-to-jaw in an ugly *rhubarb* at home plate.

5. shag—[C] practice catching in the outfield. How can Dugan text-message friends and *shag* flies at the same time?

6. moxie—[C] skill and daring. It took a lot of *moxie* for Buttermaker to pick the umpire's pocket like that.

7. Texas leaguer—[C] bloop hit. Our only base runner came courtesy of a *Texas leaguer* that plunked between two lazy fielders.

8. Baltimore chop—[A] high-bouncing ground ball. Porter is so quick, he can go from home to third before a *Baltimore chop* bounces twice.

9. fireman—[A] relief pitcher. We still think Walker is an odd name for our ace *fireman*.

10. rubber game—[B] deciding game of a series. But the southpaw did put out another fire to help us win the *rubber game* against the Knights.

11. gun down—[B] throw out a runner. Sent down to the minors, Kinsella managed to *gun down* only three out of 56 base stealers all season.

12. chin music—[B] high inside pitch. Savoy charged the mound after a little *chin music* from Wiggen.

13. gopher ball—[C] easy pitch to slug. Dutch looked more like Robert Redford in *The Natural* as he whacked my *gopher ball* into the mezzanine.

14. bang-bang—[A] close, as a play at a base. Another look in slo-mo clearly shows that the ump botched that *bang-bang* call at the plate.

15. fungo—[C] fly ball for practice. The Doc started second-guessing his rookie outfielder after watching him shag *fungoes* at spring training.

16. blow smoke—[B] throw fast. Icing down his hand, the catcher told reporters that Agilar was really *blowing smoke* tonight.

WORDS OF THE TIMES

Current events often dictate which words are looked up in online dictionaries. From merriam-webster.com, here are some terms that people frequently searched for in 2014. See the next page for answers.

1. wonk ('wonk) *n.*—A: nerdy expert. B: abject failure. C: double agent.

2. furlough ('fur-loh) *v.*—A: temporarily lay off from work. B: send long-distance. C: form a militia.

3. acerbic (a-'ser-bik) *adj.*—A: top secret. B: growing in a desert. C: sarcastic.

4. clemency ('kle-men-see) *n.*—A: petty crime. B: leniency. C: election of a pope.

5. vacuous ('va-kyoo-wus) *adj.*—A: in recess. B: empty-headed. C: irresistible.

6. austerity (aw-'ster-ih-tee) *n.*—A: heat wave. B: strict economizing. C: bitter disagreement.

7. cornucopia (kor-nuh-'koh-pee-uh) *n.*—A: trite comedy. B: abundance. C: fantastic dream.

8. bellicose ('be-lih-kohs) *adj.*—A: melodic. B: potbellied. C: warlike.

9. moniker ('mah-nih-ker) *n.*—A: milestone. B: nickname. C: stand-up comic.

10. curmudgeon (ker-'muh-jen) *n.*—A: dog breeder. B: grouch. C: knockout punch.

11. reconcile ('re-kon-siyl) *v.*—A: restore harmony. B: banish. C: put to extended use.

12. filibuster ('fi-lih-bus-ter) *v.*—A: meddle. B: round up allies. C: use tactics to delay or prevent an action.

13. capricious (ka-'prih-shus) *adj.*—A: fickle. B: wearing a hat. C: forming an island.

14. ignominious (ig-no-'mi-nee-us) *adj.*—A: disgraceful. B: lacking knowledge. C: using a false name.

15. indemnify (in-'dem-nih-fiy) *v.*—A: curse. B: imprison. C: pay for damages.

"Words of the Times" Answers

1. wonk—[A] nerdy expert. A known computer *wonk*, Mickey was recruited by a venerable tech company.

2. furlough—[A] temporarily lay off from work. Willy Wonka shut down the chocolate factory and *furloughed* the Oompa Loompas for two weeks.

3. acerbic—[C] sarcastic. On most news shows, there's more *acerbic* chitchat than there is insightful analysis.

4. clemency—[B] leniency. Bobby's lawyer asked the judge for *clemency* even though her client had been convicted of stealing billions.

5. vacuous—[B] empty-headed. As Joy gave her report on cryptozoology, she noticed a lot of *vacuous* stares.

6. austerity—[B] strict economizing. After she lost her job when her company downsized, Ann was forced to practice *austerity*.

7. cornucopia—[B] abundance. There's a *cornucopia* of coffee shops but not enough libraries.

8. bellicose—[C] warlike. Despite his *bellicose* demeanor, he's really a softy.

9. moniker—[B] nickname. Say, Woody, how did you get the *moniker* Mister Excitement?

10. curmudgeon—[B] grouch. In 12 years, that *curmudgeon* down the hall has never said good morning to me.

11. reconcile—[A] restore harmony. The Hatfields and McCoys decided to end their bitter feud and *reconcile*.

12. filibuster—[C] use tactics to delay or prevent an action. The president's opponents threatened to *filibuster* his nominee to the Supreme Court.

13. capricious—[A] fickle. Nothing is more *capricious* than New England weather.

14. ignominious—[A] disgraceful. After a promising start, the Mud Hens finished the season with an *ignominious* 100 losses.

15. indemnify—[C] pay for damages. "Somebody has to *indemnify* me for this broken window," Mr. Wilson told Dennis the Menace.

CHECK YOUR PRIDE

People often look up *hubris*, which means "overbearing pride." In ancient Greece, it conveyed an audacious attitude toward the gods. We see hubris in the story of the RMS *Titanic*, built with excessive grandeur and lost on her maiden voyage, and in Dr. Frankenstein, who presumed to acquire the power to create life. Hubris is foolish pride that leads to a fall.

AIN'T LOVE GRAND?

Love is a snowmobile racing across the tundra and then suddenly it flips over, pinning you underneath. At night, the ice weasels come.
—MATT GROENING

"

Put your hand on a hot stove for a minute, and it seems like an hour. Sit with a pretty girl for an hour, and it seems like a minute. That's relativity.
—ALBERT EINSTEIN

"

I was married by a judge. I should have asked for a jury.
—GROUCHO MARX

"

A girl phoned me the other day and said, "Come on over. There's nobody home." I went over. Nobody was home.
—RODNEY DANGERFIELD

 QUOTABLE TWEETS

I got laid at IKEA this morning. Assembling the woman took a while though.
@JUDAHWORLDCHAMP (JUDAH FRIEDLANDER)

THE PERFECT WORDS FOR

ROASTS

His mother should have thrown him
away and kept the stork.

—MAE WEST

"

[He was] one of the nicest old ladies I ever met.

—WILLIAM FAULKNER

"

He may look like an idiot and talk like an idiot,
but don't let that fool you; he really is an idiot.

—GROUCHO MARX

"

I will always love the false image I had of you.

—ASHLEIGH BRILLIANT

"

A modest little person,
with much to be modest about.

—WINSTON CHURCHILL

"

I've just learned about his illness.
Let's hope it's nothing trivial.

—IRVIN S. COBB

I do desire we may be better strangers.
—WILLIAM SHAKESPEARE

"

She tells enough white lies to ice a wedding cake.
—MARGOT ASQUITH

"

In order to avoid being called a flirt,
she always yielded easily.
—CHARLES, COUNT TALLEYRAND

"

He has no enemies, but is intensely disliked
by his friends.
—OSCAR WILDE

"

That woman speaks eighteen languages and
can't say no in any of them.
—DOROTHY PARKER

"

He loves nature in spite of what it did to him.
—FORREST TUCKER

"

There is nothing wrong with you that
reincarnation won't cure.
—JACK E. LEONARD

Turn your wounds into wisdom.
—OPRAH

WORDS OF WISDOM

The insights of the greatest minds
lead us to a deeper understanding
of the world, humankind, and ourselves.
Through the eyes of others we see new
angles that can shape our own vision.

WISDOM

Wisdom outweighs any wealth.
—SOPHOCLES

"

There is a plan to this universe. There is
a high intelligence, maybe even a purpose, but
it's given to us on the installment plan.
—ISAAC BASHEVIS SINGER

"

Common sense is not so common.
—VOLTAIRE

"

I not only use all the brains that I have,
but all that I can borrow.
—WOODROW WILSON

"

To understand a new idea, break an old habit.
—JEAN TOOMER

"

Common sense is wisdom with its sleeves rolled up.
—KYLE FARNSWORTH

"

It's the possibility of having a dream come true
that makes life interesting.
—PAUL COELHO

The man who complains about the way
the ball bounces is likely the one who dropped it.

—KENT HILL

"
You'll never have any mental muscle if you
don't have any heavy stuff to pick up.

—DIANE LANE

"
Turn your face to the sun and the
shadows fall behind you.

—JAN GOLDSTEIN

"
Never ask the barber if you need a haircut.

—WARREN BUFFETT

"
Be open to learning new lessons even if they
contradict the lessons you learned yesterday.

—ELLEN DEGENERES

 **QUOTABLE TWEETS**

True wisdom has a curious way
of revealing to yourself
your own true ignorance.

@NEILTYSON (NEIL DEGRASSE TYSON)

LIFE

Think of life as a terminal illness, because
if you do, you will live it with joy and
passion, as it ought to be lived.
—ANNA QUINDLEN

"

There are only two ways to live your life.
One is as though nothing is a miracle. The other
is as though everything is a miracle.
—ALBERT EINSTEIN

"

There are no regrets in life, just lessons.
—JENNIFER ANISTON

"

If you're quiet, you're not living. You've got to be noisy
and colorful and lively.
—MEL BROOKS

"

The first step to getting the things you want out of life is
this: Decide what you want.
—BEN STEIN

"

Big changes in our lives are more or less
a second chance.
—HARRISON FORD

You don't have to have been near death to know...
what living is all about—but maybe it helps.
—LANCE ARMSTRONG

"

Life's a roller coaster, and you never know
when it's going to take a turn.
—TY PENNINGTON

"

Life is a series of commas, not periods.
—MATTHEW MCCONAUGHEY

"

Keep moving if you love life, and keep
your troubles well behind you.
—JOHN MCCAIN

"

I don't make plans, because life is short and
unpredictable—much like the weather!
—AL ROKER

🐦 QUOTABLE TWEETS

Find a spot on Earth that is
comfortable for you.
Keep that spot clean physically
or in your mind. Think about the spot
when you are away.
@YOKOONO

TRUTH

Truth may be stranger than fiction, goes the
old saw, but it is never as strange as lies.
—JOHN HODGMAN

"

The truth needs so little rehearsal.
—BARBARA KINGSOLVER

"

Delete the adjectives and [you'll] have the facts.
—HARPER LEE

"

Bad taste is simply saying the truth before
it should be said.
—MEL BROOKS

"

If you tell the truth, you don't need a long memory.
—JESSE VENTURA

"

The pursuit of truth is like picking raspberries.
You miss a lot if you approach it from only one angle.
—RANDAL MARLIN

"

Lying makes a problem part of the future;
truth makes a problem part of the past.
—RICK PITINO

KINDNESS

Do your little bit of good where you are;
it is those little bits of good put together
that overwhelm the world.

—DESMOND TUTU

"

You cannot do a kindness too soon,
for you never know how soon it will be too late.

—RALPH WALDO EMERSON

"

A little kindness from person to person
is better than a vast love for all humankind.

—RICHARD DEHMEL

 QUOTABLE TWEETS

Every mental event has a
neural correlate.
Through mindfulness we can
rewire the brain for peace,
harmony, laughter, and love.

@DEEPAKCHOPRA

THE PERFECT WORDS FOR

PEP TALKS

It's a shallow life that doesn't
give a person a few scars.
—GARRISON KEILLOR

"

If you are not criticized, you may not be doing much.
—DONALD RUMSFELD

"

He who limps is still walking.
—STANISLAW LEC

"

He who cannot forgive others destroys the bridge
over which he himself must pass.
—GEORGE HERBERT

"

What does not kill him, makes him stronger.
—FRIEDRICH NIETZSCHE

"

Write injuries in sand, kindnesses in marble.
—FRENCH PROVERB

"

If we were born knowing everything, what would
we do with all this time on this earth?
—NELLY

WORDS TO SHARE

We are a social species. Not only do we have thousands of words to use in conversation, we also have many to describe the very act of conversing. So the next time you're confabulating,[1] try out some of these words on your interlocutor.[2] For quiz answers, turn the page.

1. gainsay *v.*—A: repeat. B: add, as an afterthought. C: deny.

2. badinage (bad-uh-'nazh) *n.*—A: swearwords. B: playful back-and-forth. C: stern warning.

3. taciturn ('tass-uh-turn) *adj.*—A: chatty. B: quiet. C: afflicted with a lisp.

4. wheedle ('wee-dull) *v.*—A: tease. B: speak breathily. C: persuade with flattery.

5. loquacious (low-'kway-shus) *adj.*—A: quick to agree. B: talkative. C: to the point.

6. wag *n.*—A: unfair debater. B: joker. C: short digression.

7. polemic (puh-'lem-ick) *n.*—A: opinionated attack. B: off-the-cuff remark. C: awkward pause.

8. schmooze ('shmooz) *v.*—A: contradict oneself. B: chat. C: mispronounce.

9. maunder ('mawn-dur or 'mahn-) *v.*—A: ramble. B: squabble. C: gurgle.

10. rodomontade (rod-uh-mun-'tayd or -'tahd) *n.*—A: circular argument. B: talking while walking. C: bragging.

11. repartee (rep-ur-'tee or -ar-'tay) *n.*—A: verbal habit, as "like" and "you know." B: witty reply. C: rhetorical question.

12. bombastic (bahm-'bass-tick) *adj.*—A: shocking. B: pompous. C: given to interrupting.

13. prevaricate (prih-'var-uh-kate) *v.*—A: scream. B: emphasize. C: tell a half-truth.

14. colloquy ('coll-uh-kwee) *n.*—A: dialogue. B: slang usage. C: translation.

15. fustian ('fuss-chun) *adj.*—A: obscure. B: high-flown. C: mumbled.

16. tête-à-tête (tet-uh-'tet) *n.*—A: comeback. B: roundtable. C: private conversation.

17. insinuate (in-'sin-yoo-ate or -ya-wayt) *v.*—A: make hand gestures. B: embellish. C: artfully suggest.

---

1. chatting   2. participant in a dialogue   *Words of Wisdom*   **193**

"Words to Share" Answers

1. gainsay—[C] deny. It cannot be *gainsaid* that the sign maker who spelled "Exit" wrong is an idiot.

2. badinage—[B] playful back-and-forth. The team's locker-room *badinage* is not for the squeamish.

3. taciturn—[B] quiet. The only *taciturn* member of a large and boisterous family, Mavis grew up to become a psychotherapist.

4. wheedle—[C] persuade with flattery. The saleswoman *wheedled* me into buying this dress.

5. loquacious—[B] talkative. My *loquacious* seatmate bent my ear all the way from LaGuardia to LAX.

6. wag—[B] joker. Ever the *wag*, Mike stood in the receiving line clutching a joy buzzer.

7. polemic—[A] opinionated attack. The meeting was interrupted by Jay's *polemic* against the copying machine.

8. schmooze—[B] chat. He doesn't know the difference between a driver and a putter—he just likes *schmoozing* at the country club.

9. maunder—[A] ramble. We listened to Uncle Horace's *maundering* stories, one right after another.

10. rodomontade—[C] bragging. The actress's Oscar acceptance speech came off as 45 seconds of unabashed *rodomontade*.

11. repartee—[B] witty reply. When Curly asked, "What's that monkey got that I ain't got?" Moe's *repartee* was "A longer tail."

12. bombastic—[B] pompous. The club president's speech would have seemed less *bombastic* without Tchaikovsky's "1812 Overture" playing in the background.

13. prevaricate—[C] tell a half-truth. When asked if he'd broken the window, the Little Leaguer *prevaricated*, claiming that as a southpaw, his aim couldn't have been that good.

14. colloquy—[A] dialogue. The professors' highbrow *colloquy* quickly turned into a slugfest.

15. fustian—[B] high-flown. The candidate's *fustian* oratory barely disguised his poor grasp of the issue.

16. tête-à-tête—[C] private conversation. After a quick *tête-à-tête* with his attorney, the defendant decided to change his plea.

17. insinuate—[C] artfully suggest. When my friends chipped in for my birthday present—a gift certificate for a housecleaning service—I had to wonder what they were *insinuating*.

SMARTY PANTS

Are you smarter than a 12th grader? We've been saving up these words—from the *Princeton Review's Word Smart: Genius Edition* test-prep guide—for our most confident quiz takers. Turn the page for answers.

1. umbrage ('um-brij) *n.*—
A: resentment. B: bright sunshine.
C: utter confusion.

2. sobriquet ('soh-brih-kay) *n.*—
A: nickname. B: tight bandage.
C: barbecue coal.

3. feckless ('fek-les) *adj.*—
A: bold and daring. B: of clear complexion. C: weak and ineffective.

4. bailiwick ('bay-lih-wik) *n.*—
A: special domain. B: holiday candle.
C: dugout canoe.

5. onus ('oh-nus) *n.*—
A: proof of residency or status.
B: burden. C: unique entity.

6. ductile ('duk-tuhl) *adj.*—
A: of plumbing. B: easily shaped or influenced. C: hard to locate or define.

7. troglodyte ('trah-glih-diyt) *n.*—
A: cave dweller or reclusive person.
B: bird of prey. C: know-it-all.

8. paean ('pee-in) *n.*—
A: fervent prayer. B: lowly worker.
C: song of praise.

9. sangfroid ('sahn-fwah) *n.*—
A: snooty attitude. B: coolness under pressure. C: French chef.

10. redoubtable (rih-'dau-te-bul) *adj.*—A: open to debate. B: famous.
C: formidable.

11. imprecate ('im-prih-kayt) *v.*—
A: accuse. B: curse. C: pester or distract.

12. modicum ('mah-dih-kum) *n.*—
A: small portion. B: middle path.
C: daily dosage.

13. somnambulist (sahm-'nam-byeh-list) *n.*—A: sleepwalker.
B: hypnotizer. C: historian.

14. restive ('res-tiv) *adj.*—
A: comfortable. B: left over.
C: fidgety.

15. anomie ('a-neh-mee) *n.*—
A: arch foe. B: mutual attraction.
C: social instability.

"Smarty Pants" Answers

1. umbrage—[A] resentment. Why did your team take such *umbrage* at being called the underdogs?

2. sobriquet—[A] nickname. Say, Paul, how did you get the *sobriquet* Grumpy?

3. feckless—[C] weak and ineffective. In formal debate, "Oh, yeah?" is a rather *feckless* rebuttal.

4. bailiwick—[A] special domain. "Ask me anything about grammar," the curmudgeonly copy editor said. "That's my *bailiwick*."

5. onus—[B] burden. "The *onus*," Mr. Peterson barked, "is on your boys to fix my broken window."

6. ductile—[B] easily shaped or influenced. Decisive? No. Tara's opinions are sometimes as *ductile* as Play-Doh.

7. troglodyte—[A] cave dweller or reclusive person. I wouldn't go so far as to call Jerry a *troglodyte*, but he's definitely on the shy side.

8. paean—[C] song of praise. Let us raise a toast and a rousing *paean* to Jay and Cathy's wedding!

9. sangfroid—[B] coolness under pressure. With unrelenting *sangfroid*, Andrea remained a pro at the poker table despite the high stakes.

10. redoubtable—[C] formidable. The pitcher shuddered as the *redoubtable* Albert Pujols strode to the plate.

11. imprecate—[B] curse. Before being banished, the witch ominously threatened to *imprecate* the town for five generations.

12. modicum—[A] small portion. All I ask is a *modicum* of cooperation with the housework.

13. somnambulist—[A] sleepwalker. For a *somnambulist*, Lady Macbeth is rather talkative.

14. restive—[C] fidgety. Peter got so *restive* during the SAT, he chewed his pencil almost to the lead.

15. anomie—[C] social instability. Apparently there's too much *anomie* in Congress for the bill to be passed.

A STROKE OF ...

Genius originally meant "guardian spirit," from the Latin *gignere* ("to beget, to produce"), and dates back to at least 1393. It's related to the words *genus, gender, generation,* and even *kin*—all suggestive of birth. The modern meaning, of a person endowed with a natural ability or talent, comes from Milton's *Iconoclastes* (1649).

ALL IN THE MIND

Don your thinking cap for this quiz on words about all matters cerebral. Feeling the brain strain? Turn the page for answers.

1. ken ('ken) *n.*—A: hunch. B: attention span. C: range of knowledge.

2. abstruse (ab-'stroos) *adj.*—A: scatterbrained. B: hard to comprehend. C: obvious to anyone.

3. cogent ('koh-jent) *adj.*—A: from a man's perspective. B: convincing. C: of two minds.

4. construe (kon-'strew) *v.*—A: interpret. B: baffle. C: refuse to believe.

5. erudition (er-uh-'di-shun) *n.*—A: clear speech. B: extensive learning through books. C: loss of memory.

6. nescient ('neh-shee- or 'neeh-see-unt) *adj.*—A: showing good judgment. B: having foresight. C: lacking knowledge.

7. sagacious (se-'gay-shus) *adj.*—A: beyond belief. B: showing insight. C: mentally stimulating.

8. métier ('me-tyay) *adj.*—A: measure of intelligence. B: doubt. C: area of expertise.

9. recondite ('re-kon- or ri-'kahn-diyt) *adj.*—A: triggering a memory. B: skeptical. C: deep or obscure.

10. untenable (un-'te-ne-bul) *adj.*—A: impossible to defend. B: not open to question. C: obtuse.

11. autodidact (aw-toh-'diy-dakt or '-dakt) *n.*—A: demanding teacher. B: complete thought. C: self-taught person.

12. empirical (im-'peer-ih-kul) *adj.*—A: all-knowing. B: widely accepted. C: from experience rather than theory.

13. polymath ('pah-lee-math) *n.*—A: teacher. B: person of great and varied learning. C: numerical puzzle.

14. cogitate ('kah-je-tayt) *v.*—A: think deeply. B: become confused. C: take a guess.

15. pundit ('pun-dit) *n.*—A: humorist. B: pupil. C: critic or airer of opinions.

"All in the Mind" Answers

1. ken—[C] range of knowledge. Sorry, but the care and feeding of anything with eight legs is a little outside my *ken*.

2. abstruse—[B] hard to comprehend. Do you find the rules of British cricket a bit *abstruse*?

3. cogent—[B] convincing. Alice did not consider the Mad Hatter's reasoning to be all that *cogent*.

4. construe—[A] interpret. It's hard to *construe* a politician's real meaning through all the bluster.

5. erudition—[B] extensive learning through books. Despite her *erudition*, Jen was prone to commonsense blunders in her love life.

6. nescient—[C] lacking knowledge. "How can you offer the contract to that *nescient* neophyte?" Dan whined.

7. sagacious—[B] showing insight. Winning Fay's heart by reciting Persian poetry was Joe's *sagacious* plan.

8. métier—[C] area of expertise. Etiquette was Emily's purported *métier*, but it certainly didn't show at the state dinner last night.

9. recondite—[C] deep or obscure. Nothing, Jimmy's mom joked, is as *recondite* as the password for her son's tree house.

10. untenable—[A] impossible to defend. The row of dug-up flower beds put Andy's new puppy in a most *untenable* position.

11. autodidact—[C] self-taught person. In the field of foot-in-mouth, unfortunately, I'm an *autodidact*.

12. empirical—[C] from experience rather than theory. Jill has *empirical* evidence that microwaving a plate full of marshmallows is not a wise idea.

13. polymath—[B] person of great and varied learning. A true *polymath*, Randi was acing every question on *Jeopardy!*

14. cogitate—[A] think deeply. "To solve this case, Watson," said Sherlock Holmes, "one must *cogitate* over a pipeful of tobacco."

15. pundit—[C] critic or airer of opinions. I'm getting swamped by all the talking-head *pundits* on TV.

SOLID FOUNDATION

They say a good vocabulary is the foundation of learning. Master these terms related to architecture and construction, and you will build yourself a fine edifice.
Answers on next page.

1. raze ('rayz) *v.*—A: build up. B: dig a foundation. C: tear down.

2. dexterous ('dek-ster-us) *adj.*— A: skillful. B: left-handed. C: turned clockwise.

3. jury-rig ('jur-ee-rig) *v.*—A: set up permanently. B: construct in a makeshift fashion. C: glaze.

4. stud ('stuhd) *n.*—A: slang for a good carpenter. B: leveling bar. C: upright post.

5. on spec (on 'spek) *adv.*— A: using blueprints. B: without a contract. C: ahead of schedule.

6. garret ('gar-it) *n.*—A: attic room. B: pantry or extra kitchen room. C: basement room.

7. annex ('a-neks) *n.*— A: supplementary structure. B: underground dwelling. C: foundation.

8. wainscot ('wayn-skoht) *n.*— A: intricate plasterwork. B: scaffolding. C: paneled part of a wall.

9. rotunda (roh-'tun-duh) *n.*— A: central column. B: circular room. C: revolving door.

10. plumb ('plum) *adj.*—A: not linked, as pipes. B: past its prime. C: vertical.

11. aviary ('ay-vee-ehr-ee) *n.*— A: house for birds. B: airport terminal. C: open lobby.

12. corrugated ('kor-eh-gayt-ed) *adj.*—A: with closed doors. B: rusted. C: having a wavy surface.

13. mezzanine ('meh-zeh-neen) *n.*—A: lowest balcony floor. B: domed ceiling. C: marble counter.

14. cornice ('kor-nes) *n.*— A: meeting of two walls. B: decorative top edge. C: steeple or spire.

15. vestibule ('ves-teh-buyl) *n.*— A: dressing room. B: lobby. C: staircase.

"Solid Foundation" Answers

1. raze—[C] tear down. I hear they're going to *raze* the mall and build a greenhouse.

2. dexterous—[A] skillful. Charlotte spun her web with amazingly *dexterous* eight-handedness.

3. jury-rig—[B] construct in a makeshift fashion. The contractors were let go after they *jury-rigged* our home's first floor.

4. stud—[C] upright post. Don't start hammering the wall until you locate a *stud* behind it.

5. on spec—[B] without a contract. Dad is building the girls' dollhouse *on spec*.

6. garret—[A] attic room. I'm not fancy—a cozy *garret* is all I need to finish the novel.

7. annex—[A] supplementary structure. The children's *annex* was a welcome addition to the library.

8. wainscot—[C] paneled part of a wall. Marge's kids have treated the entire *wainscot* as an experimental crayon mural.

9. rotunda—[B] circular room. The conflicting blueprints for the *rotunda* have me going in circles!

10. plumb—[C] vertical. Our fixer-upper may need new floors, doors, and windows, but at least the walls are *plumb*.

11. aviary—[A] house for birds. "Your cat hasn't taken his eyes off that *aviary*," Sheryl noted.

12. corrugated—[C] having a wavy surface. All we have for a roof is a sheet of *corrugated* tin.

13. mezzanine—[A] lowest balcony floor. Sadly, our $165 seats in the *mezzanine* had an obstructed view.

14. cornice—[B] decorative top edge. You're going to need one heck of an extension ladder to reach that *cornice*.

15. vestibule—[B] lobby. Anxiety peaking, Claire waited over an hour in the *vestibule* for her interview.

GARDEN VARIETY

A *trellis* is a structure of crisscross slats on which vines or flowers may climb. An *espalier* is a trellis often set against a flat wall. An *arbor* makes an arch of that trellis, and a *pergola* puts the trellis above a frame made of posts. If the structure's roof is solid instead, you have a *gazebo*. And if the gazebo is high on a hill, it may be called a *belvedere* (Italian for "beautiful view").

SOLAR POWERED

The sun has long played a role in our celebrations, so we pay homage as the sun days cycle through the year. See next page for answers.

1. pantheism *n.*—A: crossing of social boundaries. B: burying of the dead. C: belief that God and the universe are identical.

2. propitiate *v.*—A: honor. B: appease. C: revive.

3. celestial *adj.*—A: ghostlike. B: fleeting. C: relating to the heavens.

4. ascension *n.*—act of ...A: rising. B: offering. C: deferring.

5. perigee *n.*—A: layer of an atmosphere. B: point where an orbiting object is nearest to the earth. C: shift of seasons.

6. divination *n.*—A: split of harvest. B: immortality. C: supernatural insight into the future.

7. druid *n.*—A: Celtic priest. B: astrological society. C: blind follower.

8. hallowed *adj.*—A: mystical. B: respected. C: untouchable.

9. renascent *adj.*—A: warming. B: of the heart. C: rising again.

10. saltation *n.*—A: leaping or dancing. B: elaborate greeting. C: deep sleep.

11. declination *n.*—A: end of a season. B: diminished daylight. C: distance of a heavenly body from a point on the same plane as the earth's equator.

12. exuberate *v.*—A: plan precisely. B: eat with gusto. C: overflow.

13. bacchanal *n.*—A: wild, drunken revelry. B: monk's garment. C: inscription.

14. cache *n.*—A: storage place. B. prestige. C: awkward position.

15. synodic *adj.*—relating to ... A: ancient writings. B: family bonds. C: alignment of stars and planets.

16. quondam *adj.*—A: formal. B: former. C: penitent.

"Solar Powered" Answers

1. pantheism—[C] belief that God and the universe are identical. *Pantheism* demands a deep connection to nature.

2. propitiate—[B] appease. The villagers offered bushels of grain to *propitiate* the gods.

3. celestial—[C] relating to the heavens. The sparkling stars accentuated the evening's celestial majesty.

4. ascension—[A] act of rising. The morning crowd marveled at the sun's *ascension*.

5. perigee—[B] point where an orbiting object is nearest to the earth. With the moon at its *perigee*, the night sky was awash in light.

6. divination—[C] supernatural insight into the future. Lela's powers of *divination* proved eerily accurate.

7. druid—[A] Celtic priest. Mist swirled as the *druids* gathered near Stonehenge at daybreak.

8. hallowed—[B] respected. During the ceremony, even the wildest children quieted near the *hallowed* burial grounds.

9. renascent—[C] rising again. Every year, we suffer through a gray and bitter winter, eager for spring and its *renascent* light and warmth.

10. saltation— [A] leaping or

dancing. Celebrants in the throes of *saltation* were silhouetted against the bonfire.

11. declination—[C] distance of a heavenly body from a point on the same plane as the earth's equator. Tiberius used astronomy and *declination* values for navigation.

12. exuberate—[C] overflow. Vegetables *exuberated* from storage cellars after the harvest.

13. bacchanal—[A] wild, drunken revelry. The streets were thronged as prayer gave way to *bacchanal*.

14. cache—[A] storage place. The townspeople stocked *caches* with grain in anticipation of a long winter.

15. synodic—[C] relating to alignment of stars and planets. Early calendars were based on the moon's *synodic* cycle.

16. quondam—[B] former. Spying her *quondam* beau at the party, she felt relieved that he was in her past.

SHARP TALKER

You already know that staying in shape is a key to good health. But just as important: keeping your vocabulary finely tuned and toned. Try this quiz—about shapes of the literal sort—then hit the next page for answers.

1. gangling ('gan-gling) *adj.*— A: loose and lanky. B: bulging with muscles. C: short in stature.

2. helix ('hee-liks) *n.*—A: pointed tip. B: warped outline. C: spiral.

3. deltoid ('del-toyd) *adj.*— A: triangular. B: circular. C: squared off.

4. trefoil ('tree-foyl) *adj.*— A: pliable. B: having a three-leaf design. C: tapering narrowly.

5. conical ('kah-nih-kul) *adj.*— A: like an igloo. B: like a cone. C: like a tunnel.

6. pentacle ('pen-tih-kul) *n.*— A: star. B: crescent moon. C: square.

7. elliptical (ih-'lip-tih-kul) *adj.*— A: slanted. B: embossed. C: oval.

8. sigmoid ('sig-moyd) *adj.*— A: crossed like an X. B: curved like a C or an S. C: bent like an L.

9. whorl ('hworl) *n.*—A: well-rounded muscle. B: flat surface. C: circular pattern.

10. serrated ('seh-rayt-ed) *adj.*— A: interconnected, as with circles or rings. B: elongated. C: having notched edges.

11. cordate ('kor-dayt) *adj.*— A: stringlike. B: heart shaped. C: free-form.

12. svelte ('svelt) *adj.*– A: undulating. B: lean. C: in a checked or repeating pattern.

13. zaftig ('zaf-tig) *adj.*— A: pleasingly plump. B: moldable, like putty. C: seedlike, as in an avocado or a peach.

14. lozenge ('lah-zunj) *n.*— A: 90-degree angle. B: level used in architectural design. C: diamond.

15. ramify ('ra-meh-fiy) *v.*— A: become solid, as cement. B: jut out. C: split into branches or parts.

"Sharp Talker" Answers

1. gangling—[A] loose and lanky. The protagonist of "The Legend of Sleepy Hollow" was the *gangling* pedagogue.

2. helix—[C] spiral. Judy is a DNA researcher, so she's getting a tattoo of a double *helix*.

3. deltoid—[A] triangular. The pyramids' architects obviously knew a thing or two about the stability of *deltoid* structures.

4. trefoil—[B] having a three-leaf design. The gardening club uses a *trefoil* symbol—a gilded clover— as its logo.

5. conical—[B] like a cone. My favorite *conical* item? Why, the ice-cream cone, of course, topped preferably with three scoops of chocolate.

6. pentacle—[A] star. Hey, this tarot deck is missing all the cards with *pentacles*!

7. elliptical—[C] oval. Just two times around the *elliptical* running track, and Rebecca was wiped out.

8. sigmoid—[B] curved like a C or an S. On Superman's chest sits a single scarlet *sigmoid* symbol.

9. whorl—[C] circular pattern. To find the treasure, take 50 paces east from the tree with the *whorl* in its trunk.

10. serrated—[C] having notched edges. "I'm not sure that old *serrated* knife is best for carving the turkey," Dad advised.

11. cordate—[B] heart shaped. Sarah is baking *cordate* cookies for her cardiologist boyfriend.

12. svelte—[B] lean. The holidays pose a serious challenge to my *svelte* frame!

13. zaftig—[A] pleasingly plump. Known for her *zaftig* figure, Caroline was a surprising choice for the fashion magazine's debut cover.

14. lozenge—[C] diamond. The boys dug up the grass to create a makeshift *lozenge* so they could play ball.

15. ramify—[C] split into branches or parts. "We need to *ramify* this department to keep productivity high!" Kerrie emphasized at yesterday's staff meeting.

WHAT'S THE ANGLE?

In geometry, you find various shapes called *polygons*, from the Greek *poly-* for "many" plus *gonia* for "angle." Hence, a pentagon has five angles (and sides), a hexagon has six, a heptagon has seven, an octagon has eight, and so on.